DREAD TALK

THE LANGUAGE OF RASTAFARI

Revised Edition

VELMA POLLARD

Canoe Press
Barbados • Jamaica • Trinidad and Tobago

McGill-Queen's University Press
Montreal & Kingston • London • Chicago

Revised edition 2000
Published simultaneously by
McGill-Queen's University Press (worldwide except the Caribbean)
ISBN 978-0-7735-2030-1 (paper)
ISBN 978-0-7735-6828-0 (ePDF)
Legal deposit second quarter 2000
Bibliothèque nationale du Quebec
and Canoe Press University of the West Indies

Printed in Canada on acid-free paper that is 100% ancient forest free (100% post-consumer recycled),
processed chlorine free
Reprinted 2003, 2009, 2018

Funded by the · Financé par le
Government · gouvernement
of Canada · du Canada

Canada Council · Conseil des arts
for the Arts · du Canada

We acknowledge the support of the Canada Council for the Arts, which last year invested
$153 million to bring the arts to Canadians throughout the country.

Nous remercions le Conseil des arts du Canada de son soutien. L'an dernier, le Conseil a investi 153 millions de
dollars pour mettre de l'art dans la vie des Canadiennes et des Canadiens de tout le pays.

CATALOGUING IN PUBLICATION DATA
(University of the West Indies)
Pollard, Velma
Dread talk: the language of Rastafari/Velma Pollard
p. cm.
Partial contents: the road of the Dread/Lorna Goodison.
Includes bibliographical references.
ISBN 976-8125-68-3
Creole dialects, English – Jamaican. 2. Ras Tafari Movement – Language (New words, slang, etc.).
3. Jamaican dialect. I. Title.
P7874.J3P64 2000 819.82-dc20

CATALOGUING IN PUBLICATION DATA
Pollard, Velma
Dread talk: the language of Rastafari
Rev. Ed.
Includes bibliographical references.
ISBN 978-0-7735-2030-1 (paper)
ISBN 978-0-7735-6828-0 (ePDF)
Creole dialects, English – Jamaica. 2. Creole dialects, English – West Indies. 3. Rastafari movement.
4. Jamaican poetry – History and criticism. I. Title.
PM7874.J3P65 2000   427'.97292   C99-901496-X

The respective authors and publishers have generously given permission to use extended quotations
or materials from articles by the author: Excerpt from "Mabrak" by Bongo Jerry (*Savacou* 3/4).
Copyright 1980 by Bongo Jerry.
Chapter 1: *Carribean Quarterly* 26, no. 4. Copyright 1980 by Caribbean Quarterly.
Chapter 2: *Caribbean Quarterly* 28, no. 4. Copyright 1982 by Caribbean Quarterly and renewed 1983
by Society for Caribbean Linguistics (*Studies in Caribbean Language*).
Chapter 3: *York Papers in Linguistics* 11 (July 1984).
Chapter 3: *From Commonwealth to Post-Colonial,* edited by Anna Rutherford. Copyright 1992 by
Anna Rutherford.
Sections of the present work also appear in Pollard's "The speech of the Rastafarians of Jamaica,
in the Eastern Caribbean: The Case of St Lucia," *International Journal of the Sociology
of Language* 85 (1990).

For Pauline Christie,
who turned the study towards language,

and John Rickford,
who insisted on its publication

Contents

Mabrak

...
Every knee
must bow
Every tongue
confess
Every language
express
W
O
R
D
W
O
R
K
S

You

MUST

COME

TO RAS

MABRAK,

Enlightening is BLACK
hands writing the words of
black message
for black hearts to feel.

MABRAK is righting the wrongs and brain-whitening – HOW?
Not just by washing out the straightening and wearing
dashiki t'ing:

MOSTOFTHESTRAIGHTENINGISINTHETONGUE – SO HOW?

–BONGO JERRY 1970

Foreword to the First Edition

In *Dread Talk*, Velma Pollard not only introduces "a discussion on the language that has evolved … particularly on the lexical items that have emerged as a result of the impact of the movement on the Jamaican speech situation", but also offers what may in time be a seminal work of importance to Caribbean lexical classification. If "siin aiya" translates, as she informs us it does, "Yes brother, I agree with you", then this represents just one example of a category of lexical items that bear new meanings for listeners from non-Rastafarian constituencies. There are also words which bear the weight of their phonological implications though in need of explanation for understanding. "Downpress" which is used for "oppress" makes more sense to the Rasta man, then, since if one is being pressed (weighted) down by the injustice and marginality of his Babylonian captivity, this pressure cannot possibly be "up" (sc. "op").

The play on words – a Jamaican facility that extends from theatrical punning to everyday speech – is artlessly embraced by the Rastafarians in the repertoire of "I" (ai) words which Mrs Pollard indicates will, on closer examination, disclose that "ai" is not merely used as a pronominal form to replace the Jamaican Creole "mi" but is also used as prefix to some nouns as replacement for the initial sound in any number of words of varying function in a sentence. So "declaration" in the phrase "Declaration of Human Rights" becomes "aik-lerieshan" … according to Mrs Pollard. The relationship of the lexical formulations to a social context of economic deprivation, powerlessness and cultural subjugation is only hinted at (this not being the main thrust of her paper) but Mrs Pollard rightly informs the reader that "the reaction of the class-room teacher, like the reaction of the middle-class parent, is perhaps less a reaction to any linguistic threat than to the social impact of a movement they fear and do not understand". The Rastafarian movement in defiance of a society perceived as oppressive (downpressing) defies the society's language. "Ai man a penetrat something els" is an eloquent sampling of the easy admixture of Jamaican Creole and Dread Talk. It means in Jamaican Standard English "I was thinking deeply about something else."

REX NETTLEFORD

Preface

Even in Jamaican society, Rastafarianism is a unique phenomenon, in that it appears unrelated to European or even African cultural antecedents. Part of this unique quality is a distinctively different attitude towards the world and man's place in that world. The popularly known aspects of Rastafari – dreadlocks, smoking ganja and reggae music – appeal to many precisely because they seem so different. But one needs to go beyond a superficial appreciation of these features to understand the different attitudes. An understanding of Rastafarian speech is necessary for this appreciation. Far from being simply a dialect of English or an anglophone Creole (or just a variant of Jamaican patois), "Dread Talk" reflects the speaker's resistance to perceived oppression (both historical colonial prejudice and current economic disenfranchisement) and the sense of the overwhelming potential spiritual redemption that Rastas can achieve. Here patterns of speech really do reflect patterns of thought.

This book focuses on the importance of language to Rastafarians, and any study of this "unofficial" Jamaican religion would be incomplete without a thorough reading of it. This collection of papers, originally published in 1994 by Canoe Press, University of the West Indies, now includes a new chapter and a bibliography. The new chapter takes into account some recent developments in what can only be termed the "globalization" of Rasta culture, much of it represented on the Internet.

This latest version is a joint publication between Canoe Press and McGill-Queen's University Press. Sociolinguists, as well as historians and anthropologists, will find this book a detailed and sensitive study of a New World, twentieth century socioreligious movement.

The first of the papers in this collection was originally published in a Caribbean Quarterly (CQ) volume *Rastafari* (1985). Subsequent papers were published in CQ as well. All but the most recent paper (chapter 6) have been presented at conferences, chiefly of the Society for Caribbean Linguistics (SCL). Chapter 2 appears in the SCL 1983 publication *Studies in Caribbean Language*.

Chapter 1 starts with an introduction to Dread Talk and its relationship with Jamaican Creole. Three major categories of processes of word formation are defined. In the first, common words bear new meanings (/soundz/ means the word you hear that may not have the meaning you think); in the second, words carry their phonological meaning (/ovastan/ from "understand" because to truly *under*stand an idea you must be *over* it); and in the third, initial consonants or syllables are replaced with the sound /ai/, for example, "researched" becomes /aisercht/. What is clear is that these categories, while they serve the reader well in giving a basis from which some understanding of Dread Talk can be gained, also bring the realization that many words carry double and sometimes triple meanings. Later chapters provide an important explanation of the sociohistorical background in which these meanings have developed. Chapter 2 is particularly strong in this regard, and here a fourth category of word definitions is added under "New Items". Words such as "Atops", "spliff" and "deaders" take on seemingly unrelated meanings of "Red Stripe Beer", "marijuana cigarette" and "meat", respectively.

Chapter 3 examines the differences and similarities between Dread Talk in St Lucia and Barbados and how the spread of this language allows lexical changes that are both externally and internally generated. Chapter 4 explores the relationship between Dread Talk and modern Jamaican poetry. Chapter 5 examines how Standard Jamaican English, the official national language, has been affected by Dread Talk.

Chapter 6 is a discussion of the sociological and linguistic implications of Rasta dictionaries available on the Internet, as well as other publications. Here the wordmaking process is revisited and *transculturación*, a term which reflects another aspect of the globalization of Rasta culture, is introduced. The conclusion is that variations in Dread Talk are inherent in this type of cultural "exchange" and are bound to move the language into new, unanticipated spheres.

DREAD TALK

Dread Talk – The Speech of the Rastafari in Jamaica[1]

Introduction

The history and sociology of the Rastafari in Jamaica have been the subject of enough literature[2] to legitimize Rex Nettleford's comment that the movement is "one of the most significant phenomena to emerge out of the modem history and sociology of Plantation America, that New World culturesphere of which Jamaica and the Caribbean are a part."[3] This chapter introduces a discussion on the language that has evolved and particularly on the lexical items that have emerged as a result of the impact of the movement on the Jamaican speech situation.[4] It is necessary, however, to restate the sociohistorical fact that the early Rastafari

---

1 Most of the transcriptions used as examples of Dread Talk in this chapter are taken from tapes of discussions between Barry Chevannes, research fellow, Institute of Social and Economic Research (ISER), University of the West Indies (UWI), Mona, Jamaica, and groups of Rastafari. Thanks are due to Mr Chevannes and to the ISER for permission to use the tapes.

2 For perhaps the earliest and still, in some ways, the most respected of these, certainly the most frequently referred to in the tapes at my disposal, see Smith, Augier, and Nettleford 1960.

3 Owens (1976), *Dread –The Rastafarians of Jamaica.*

4 Earlier attempts to treat this aspect of the Rastafarian movement are found in Owens (1976), "Note on Rastafarian Language", 64–8; Chevannes (1976, 189–94); and Peart (1977).

were predominantly poor black urban folk – since this accounts in part for the close relationship between what emerges as Rasta Talk or Dread Talk (DT) and Jamaica Creole (JC), a relationship that is close enough for me to view its development as an example of lexical expansion within a Creole System.

Jamaica Creole has traditionally been the speech form of the Jamaican poor. Education and exposure to the middle class with its Standard English aspirations has accounted for the JC/SJE (Standard Jamaican English) continuum which has become a commonplace in describing the Jamaican language situation. But the sociopolitical image which the poor black man, in this case the Rasta man, has had of himself in a society where lightness of skin tone, economic competence and certain social privileges have traditionally gone together must be included in any consideration of Rastafarian words. For the man who is making the words is a man looking up from under, a man pressed down economically and socially by the establishment. His speech form represents an attempt to bend the lexicon of Jamaica Creole to reflect his social situation and his religious views.

Dread Talk and Jamaica Creole

It is to my mind a simplistic and perhaps panic-inspired notion that Dread Talk is replacing English as the language of the young people of Jamaica. But this has become not only drawing-room talk but the serious reaction of some of the teachers in our schools. Inherent in this fear is the misconception that English was ever the language of Jamaican youth. If it had been, then some of the more unbelievable punishments for the use of Jamaica Creole (Patwa) in middle-class homes – suffered by children of parents who themselves used JC with their friends less than a generation ago – would have been unnecessary.

What seems to be developing is a certain lexical expansion to accommodate a particular, and for some people a more accurate, way of seeing life in Jamaican society. The structural relationship between JC and DT can be verified by the examination of any Rastafarian speech act. The following is an extract from a taping of an open session of "reasoning" near the University of the West Indies campus at Mona:

/ai nuo se dem piipl ier nuo a sobstanshal amownt bout empara iel silasi fers/ yu no siit/ jos bikaa dem piipl si tu it se dem nuo waa gwaan eena ert/	I know that these people here know a substantial amount about Emperor Haile Selassie, don't you see? Just because these people see to it that they know what is going on in the world.[5]

If we examine this speech act for some of the more common hallmarks of creole structure, we will probably decide it falls somewhere near the middle of our hypothetical JC/SJE continuum. Note for example that /ier/ is preferred to the JC /ya/ and note also the use of the term "substantial", a very SJE usage. But the classical JC forms are there: there is the auxiliary omission /yu no siit/; there is the /a/ representing the continuous marker /waa gwaan/; there is the pluralizer /dem/ and the complimentizer /se/. This quotation illustrates a number of points. One is that DT speakers use the continuum in much the same way as the average JC speaker, codeshifting where they will or can, a tendency that will become even more evident as additional quotations are examined in this chapter. Another point is that the phonological rendering of the /a/ is that used at the JC end of the continuum. My own comment on the importance of that sound in JC has already been made elsewhere[6] and if, as I

---

5 For the use of this particular tape, thanks are due to Dr E. Kamau Brathwaite of the Department of History, UWI, Mona.

6 Pollard, (1978) "Code Switching in Jamaica Creole – Some Educational Implications", *Caribbean Journal of Education* 5, nos. 1 & 2, p. 25.

believe, it is a sound that the uneducated JC speaker imagines not to exist in Standard English then there is every reason for DT to maintain this sound. In fact it could well be that the middle-class convert easily singles it out as a kind of talisman of JC and so must perfect it in his speech form. Alternatively, this may be one sound that the SJE speaker who speaks little JC at home perfects more easily than others. See Appendix I, a reading of Psalm 11 by an official of one Rastafarian group, accompanied by the text it represents.[7] This example makes the point more clearly than any description I could possibly attempt. Two items in the extract are unusual in the JC context: /siit/ as in /yu no siit/[8] where JC prefers /yu no si/ and the pronominal /ai/ where JC would prefer /mi/. While the stress in /siit/ representing the essentially SJE retention of the final consonant is remarkable, an explanation may well be possible, similar to that advanced for the /ai/ phenomenon which will be treated in some detail later.

It is not intended to suggest that the extreme rendering of JC phonology or even the lexical expansion of JC items is necessarily self-conscious. Language emerges to describe behaviour and eventually defines itself in certain shapes. On the subject of Rastafarian speech, Nettleford comments:

> the relexification of African forms into the language of the masters was a political necessity as well as a matter of communicative convenience but this fact of development never did deprive the slave or his creole descendants of the memory of ancestral language patterns or his skill to creatively forge new means of expression using those very patterns ... The Rastafarians are inventing a language, using existing elements to be sure, but creating a means of communication that would

---

7 See note 5 above.

8 This is a very common, affirmative phrase, sometimes replaced by /no truu/ or /rait/.

faithfully reflect the specificities of their experience and perception of self, life and the world.[9]

Thus speaks the researcher, the academic commentator. Brother W, on the other hand, one of the researched, has a more simplistic but perhaps more real explanation for the emergence of the speech patterns:

> It just arise in conversation, describing many things, or several times you have several different types of reasoning and you step up with the words ... so we the Rastas suppose to speak, that here, there and anywhere we find ourselves, we suppose to speak and no one know what we speak beside ourself. That's how we get to start.[10]

What Brother W describes as "step(ping) up" with the words is in my view a very accurate comment on what actually happens to JC words in DT. I will deal with only three categories of these words, the latest of which is the most common and the most complex and so will have to admit subcategories. The first consists of a short list of words which, when juxtaposed with their JC or SJE equivalents (for the lexicon of these two is more frequently than not the same), will be seen to include visual perspective not evident in JC items and requiring, in the case of SJE, modifiers to give the same impression. The second is a list of words whose phonology is made to bear the precise burden of meaning. The final category, that of /ai/ words, will be followed by a continuous passage meant to illustrate the effect of all these changes on the actual extended rendering of DT. You will note that, inevitably, certain items have multiple meanings

---

9 Owens 1976, iv.
10 Chevannes 1977.

and multiple syntactic functions. The term "Dread", for example, which with a particle simply means a Rastafari, is used accurately in all the following sentences:

/tingz dred iina jamdown now/	Things are very bad in Jamaica now.
/bwai dat dred/	Boy that's terrible!
e/ laik yu dred op/	Hi, it seems you have allowed your beard and hair to grow!

Category I

In which known items bear new meanings

/chant/ discuss; talk about religious matters, usually to the accompaniment of Niabinghi drums	
/faawod/ leave, go	/ai man a faawod/ I am leaving now.
/krowniet/ crown	/ ... ier tu selibriet di die di empara krowniet/ ... here to celebrate the day on which the emperor was crowned.
/riizn/ discuss; talk, synonymous with /chant/ but without drums	/wi no kyan jos riizn/ tel enitaim yu fain di spirit muuv/ Perhaps we can just talk till whenever you feel the spirit moving you (to go).
/sait/ see; identify	/now wen ai an ai shoun di bredrin dat di werk im saitin op tu du widin di buks/ duoz taimz av alredi paas/ Now when I show the brother that the work he is identifying to be done in the world of books (academic) those times are already gone ...

/siin/ yes, I agree

/siin aiya/ Yes brother, I agree with you.

/stiep/ leave; go; synonymous with /faawod/

/ai man a stiep/ I am leaving now.

/trad/ walk; travel

/now wat iz a itiopyan wie dong de/ a trad go a Jerusilem go wership fa/ Now why should an Ethiopian, from way down there be going to Jerusalem to worship?

/trad/ go through, explain

/wa di fers paat yu wud a laik ai man fi trad iin/ What is the first part you would like me to explain to you?

/sounz/ words; not necessarily their intention

/ ... nuo se di sounz dat jenklman now yuus/ nat tu ai ... / Know that the words that gentleman just used are not seriously meant for you.

/baal ed/ bald; with little hair; non-Rasta

*/ ... ai ar di dred/ and yu ar a baal ed/ ai priez di livin an yu priez di ded/ I am a Rastafari and you are not; I worship the living (God) and you worship the dead one.

/babilan/ Babylon

/dats wai jerimaia fifti wan se/ ai shal sen famin iinto babilan/ That is why Jeremiah fifty-one says I shall send famine into Babylon.

/babilan/ Babylon; policeman

*/den kiem a babilan/ fi pik op ai man/ Then came a policeman to arrest me.

/dred/; /dredlaks/ person with hair uncut; Rastafarian

See example for /baal ed/ above.

The examples with asterisks (*) are from a pop song popular on the radio and jukeboxes. The point will later be made that the record is the medium through which much of the subconscious change of lexical items takes place in the mind, rather than the speech, of youth (yuutman).

Note also that words like /chant/, /riizn/ and /trad/ are Biblical words brought back to current usage.

Category II

Words that bear the weight of their phonological implications with some explanations.

/ublain/

the University and all the people there. Note that the University of the West Indies (UWI) was formerly a College of London University, hence University College of the West Indies (UCWI). In the eyes of Rasta they have not seen the truth and so are blind.

/blainjaret/

cigarette. Note again the phone "see" /a so wi kaal it yu nuo/ blainjaret/.

/ovastan/

used for understand, for if you are in control of an idea, you must stand over it.

/dounpres/

used for oppress; for if you are being pressed down as the poor Rasta man usually sees himself to be, this pressure cannot be UP ... /weda di man did blak ar wait/ an im dounpres mi now/ iz stil siem ai a bon/ (Whether the man is black or white and he oppresses me I am still the one suffering).

Category III /ai/ words

The pronoun "I" of SJE gives place to /mi/ in JC and is glossed as I, my, mine, me, according to the context. It is this "I" of SJE that has become the predominant sound in the Rastafarian language, though its implications are far more extensive than the simple SJE pronoun "I" could ever bear. Father Owens suggests that the rejection of the JC /mi/ is the result of a perception that sees "the pronoun 'me' as expressive of subservience, as representative of the selfdegradation that was expected of the slaves by their masters ... As a consequence the pronoun 'I' has a special importance to Rastas and is expressly opposed to the servile 'me' in the singular ('I') or the plural ('I an I') ... or the reflexive ('Iself, Ian Iself ... ')."[11]

Whether Father Owens' judgement is accurate or not, what is clear from listening to any extended Rastafarian discourse is that the sequence /ai/ continually recurs. A closer examination of the usage shows that /ai/ is not used merely as a pronominal form to replace the JC /mi/ but is used as well as prefix to some nouns and as a replacement for the initial sound in any number of words of varying functions in the sentence. My own observations so far make me wary of suggesting that any rules govern the placing of the /ai/ sound – why some initial sounds remain and others are replaced may be a feature that time and further generalization of usgae dictate. Note for example in some sentences offered as earlier examples that a speaker begins with his /ai/ words and later lapses into regular JC forms. It is also true to say that both Father Owens and Barry Chevannes, who make the point that /ai an ai/ is a plural form, are not completely accurate. It seems more likely to my mind that, as in JC, where there is one form that corresponds sometimes with the singular, sometimes the plural, of SJE, so in DT there is one

---

11 Owens 1976, 65.

form that must bear the burden of the singular or the plural. It is possible that eventually an equivalent for the JC /dem/ will evolve to become the DT pluralizer. Certainly if /ai and ai/ is accepted as plural, certain DT sentences become nonsense words.

/ai/ Pronominal Function

/ai and ai taakin tu di ai ier/ an telin di man dat di king av kings liiv diiz dakument ier ... /

I have been talking to this man and telling him that the king of kings has left these documents here.

/far ai an ai ier stil av bin maaterd/ ai an ai nuo ai duo waant gon/

For although I have been martyred here, I know I don't want a gun.

/denfram di taim now ai an ai waakin wid ai an ai opan wi shuolda/ an wi get biitn far it ... /

Then from the time that we have been walking with our religion on our shoulders and we have been beaten (made to suffer) for it ...

Other sentences cited as examples of different phenomena will invariably involve a number of cases in which the unmarked pronoun must be interpreted according to context. Bear in mind also that the oral situation demands far less attention to details of number than does the written.

Initial Consonant or Syllable Replacements

/aisercht/

/siin ai an ai hav alredi aisercht/ (Seeing that I have already been researched ...)

/ailektid/

/ai an ai nuo di king alredi az ailektid/ an ambasada ier we diil wid di welfier av di piipl/ (I know that the king has already selected an ambassador here to deal with the welfare of the people)

/aimaanz/

/ai an ai naa beg dat/ ai an ai a aimaanz it/
(I am not requesting that; I am demanding it)

/aiklerieshan/

... avuman raitz/
(Declaration of Human Rights)

/aiowa/

/iz widin aiowa now dat ai gwai get nalij/
(It is in our time now that you will get knowledge)

/aidrin/

/aidrin/ didn di universiti kom among os aredi/
(Brethren, didn't the University [representatives] come among us before?)

/aidrin/

/di uondli chaaj dat ai an ai az a rasta aidrin av/ is di erb/ siin/ ai duo av no mo chaaj/
(The only charge [by the police] that I, as a Rastafari, have is the herb [you see I have no other offence])

/aizaya/

/medikal man frii/ dem kyaa kyari ed amount dem aizaya aa giit tu man az priskripshan/
(Medical men are free; they can carry any amount [of ganja] they desire and give it to people as pre-scription)

/airi/

/ja se ai an ai mos tes di man wen dem kom tu al an ai/ an nuo wat airi dwel in dem/
(Jah [Jehovah] says that I must test men when they come to me; to see what truth is in them)

/airi/

also used as a response to suggest that one agrees with a speaker – cf. /siin aiya/ /airi/ airi/ truu/ truu/

/aital/

used to describe Rastafarian food rather in the way Kosher describes Jewish; prepared in a special (and natural) way

Below is a brief extract from the chanting/reasoning

/iel rastafari/
/wan vais/
... ai an ai shuon di brejrin dat di werk dat im saitin op tu du widin di buks/ duoz taim av alredi paas/ an ai an ai av shuon im/ dat di cherch kounsl/ iz dem supuoz tu riili miit ai an ai/ tu aistablish dis ting ierso now/ rait/ an bai iz uon admishan/ in dem self dem duon av eni yuniti so ai an ai sait den se soch man ai an ai man hav mongs izrel/ chaantin tu ai an ai/ ai an ai wudn tern dem we/ yet wen ai an ai dredlaks iivn chaant/ a se/ dat di man now iz a spai an a trieta/ rait ... so wen yu kom now tu ai an ai dredlaks/ yu hafi tek wat sounz yu get/ bikaaz yu av aan di shiep/ rait/ an di fiichaz/ av a biis/ rait/ wen di man dred op widin sertin nalij now/ den ai an ai kyan aksep di man az a man hu tek di step tuwaadz integrity rait/ av di king av kingz/ av di aiternal wan av krieshan ...

Hail Rastafari
One Voice
I am showing the brethren that the work that he is now seeing indicated in the books, that he should do, should have been done a long time ago. And I have shown him that it is the church council that should meet me to establish this thing here and now (right?). And he him-self admits that they have no unity among them. So if such a man came among us communing with us, I wouldn't turn him away even when I, dreadlocks, suggest that he might be a spy and a traitor. You have to take whatever reaction you get here because you have the shape and the features of the beast. When, however, you "dread up" (grow your hair) and acquire certain knowledge then I can accept you as someone who has taken a step towards the integrity of the king of kings, of the eternal one of creation.

Conclusion

The examples used to illustrate actual usage of lexical items in the speech of the Rastafari may have offered, in addition, an indication of the context within which JC/SJE words have been "stepped up". They are used in a world which is in contradisposition to constituted religion (here symbolized by all branches of the Established Church), to the establishment and constituted authority with its laws which, in many instances, run contrary to the Rastafarian preferred way of life, and to a society in which, for a number of social, economic, and historical reasons, Rastas feel they have little stake. The effect of this view of life, and the words that define it, on the thinking – and specifically on the speech – of a new generation brought up in a society of almost obscene economic extremes (and increasingly conscious of it) cannot be dealt with effectively in this chapter.

It is necessary to point out, however, that the Reggae music which is perhaps the single most important and most constant influence on Jamaican young people is music written essentially by Rastafari and contains lyrics that, for them, are serious "messages". While the Children of Israel create words and music, the Children of Babylon are by no means deaf. So that the youth who in previous years spoke Patwa (JC) for peer group acceptance with or without their parents' assent, today effortlessly speak the same language but deeply laced with DT phrases and lexical items.

"Iman a step" as a farewell indication and "seen" for assent or "seen?" for question are commonplace in any youth talk. The phonological accuracy or the ability to sustain the items will differ from youth to youth but the forms are there. "No men allowed here" is a legend I read on a teenage boy's bedroom door. Note that this sentence is an SJE sentence but "men" (which the ignoring of the English plural in JC and DT has freed for other meaning) signifies in DT a "bad" man –

as in the comment of a rural Rasta telling his life story /a men kit ai onkl/ A MEN killed my uncle – and has come to mean for that youth (man) a homosexual.

The reaction of the classroom teacher, like the reaction of the middle-class parent, is perhaps less a reaction to any linguistic threat than to the social impact of a movement they fear and do not understand. It is true, however, that it is the linguistic manifestation that most impinges on consciousness. One may have to leave home to see an obvious Rasta (or look at the TV) but when the youth at home and the pupil in the classroom simulate the man, it is a more difficult matter to deal with. It could be that the fourth grader's excuse for his inattentiveness – /ai man a penitriet something els/ "I was thinking deeply about something else" – elicits a reaction from his teacher that is less to his language than to the social phenomenon it signifies.

Appendix 1

Christ, the Coming King

1 Why do the nations rage, and the peoples imagine a vain thing?
2 The Kings of the earth set themselves, and the rulers take counsel together, against the Lord, and against his anointed, saying,
3 Let us break their bands asunder and cast away their cords from us.

4 He who sitteth in the heavens shall laugh; the Lord shall have them in derision.
5 Then shall he speak unto them in his wrath, and vex them in his great displeasure.
6 Yet have I set my king upon my holy hill of Zion.
7 I will declare the decree: The Lord hath said unto me, Thou art my Son; this day have I begotten thee.
8 Ask of me, and I shall give thee the nations for thine inheritance, and the uttermost parts of the earth for thy possession.
9 Thou shalt break them with a rod of iron; thou shalt dash them in pieces like a potter's vessel.
10 Be wise now, therefore, O ye kings; be instructed, ye judges of the earth.
11 Serve the Lord with fear, and rejoice with trembling.
12 Kiss the Son, lest he be angry, and ye perish from the way, when his wrath is kindled but a little. Blessed are all they who put their trust in Him.

/wai duu di iiden riej/ an di piipl imajin a vien ting/
/di kingz av di ert set demself/ an di ruulaz tiek kounsl tugyeda/ agiens di laad/ an iz anaintid sein/

/ekskuuz ai/ let os brick dier banz asonda/ an kyaas awie dier kaadz fram os/

/ii dat sitet in di evn shal laaf/ di laad shal av dem in dirijan/

/den shal ii spiik tu dem in iz raat/ an veks dem in iz suor displeja/

/yet av ai set mai king opan mai oli il av zaian/
/ai wil diklier dikrii/ di laad ad sed antu mii/ dow art mai son/ dis die av ai bigatn dii/
/aks av mii an ai shal giv dii di hiiden far dain ineritans an di utamuos paat av di ert/ far dai poseshan/

/dow shal brick dem wit a rad av aian/ dow shal dash dem in piisiz laik a pataz vesi/
/bii waiz dierfuor now o ii kingz/ bii instroktid/ ii jojiz av di ert/
/serv di laad wid fier an rijais wid tremblin/
/kis di son/ les ii bii angri/ an ii perish fram di wie/ an iz raat iz kingld/ bot a likl/ blesed bii aal dem dat put dier trus/ in im/ silasi ai/ dier en mai likl puoshan av riidin/

2

The Social History
of Dread Talk

Introduction

The notion that language should not be separated from its social context has become a commonplace in recent linguistic research. This notion is nowhere more important than in the study of creole languages, whose very existence has been the result of historical phenomena determining certain social necessities. Dread Talk is a comparatively recent adjustment of the lexicon of Jamaica Creole to reflect the religious, political and philosophical positions of the believers in Rastafari.[1] Its earliest expression was within this closed group; its use was highly selective (available only to those who shared particu-

---

1 Simpson 1970, iv sums up the doctrines of the movement as follows:
  "Six doctrines stand out in the Ras Tafari belief system. The first is that black men, reincarnations of the ancient Israelites, were exiled to the West Indies because of their transgressions. Second, the wicked white man is inferior to the black man. Third, the Jamaican situation is a hopeless Hell; Ethiopia is Heaven. Fourth, Haile Selassie is the Living God. Fifth, the invincible Emperor of Abyssinia will soon arrange for expatriated persons of African descent to return to the Homeland. Sixth, in the near future black men will get revenge by compelling white men to serve them" (209–10).
  Smith et al. 1960 see the fourth of these as the only doctrine common to all the Brethren and comment: "Beyond this point the religious beliefs of Ras Tafari brethren diverge widely."

lar beliefs). The language was in fact "organic" to this movement, not only in the sense in which Nettleford (1978)
describes the movement itself but in a truly Rastafarian linguistic sense that the word was the "organ" of the movement.

Today Dread Talk functions far beyond the boundaries of
the closed group for which it designed itself. This chapter
looks at the process of its extension. But in order to appreciate the language that grew out of a need for a particular
expression, it is necessary to understand the social, historical
and philosophical contexts within which the movement that
identified the need has developed in Jamaica.

The Rastafari – Social Context

The Rastafarian community history looks to Alexander Bedward[2] and to Marcus Garvey[3] as father heroes. The crowning of Ras Tafari as Emperor Haile Selassie of Ethiopia in
November 1930 served to invite "certain Jamaicans of a Gar-
veyite persuasion" to try to interpret Garvey's words, "Look
to Africa, when a black king shall be crowned, for the day of
deliverance is near", and to identify a number of texts in
their bibles which seemed to point to Haile Selassie as the
expected "conquering lion of the tribe of Judah" (Smith et al.
1960). To Alexander Bedward revivalist and healer is attributed the statement: "Hell will be your portion if you do not
rise up and crush the white man ... there is a white wall and
a black wall and the white wall has been closing around the
black wall but now the black wall is becoming bigger than
the white and they must knock the white wall down."[4] The

---

2 Jamaican Revivalist of the nineteen twenties. For detailed report and comment
see Chevannes 1971 and Elkins 1977.

3 One of Jamaica's national heroes. For a "factual exposition" on Garvey see
Edwards 1967.

environment in which these heroes, the one spiritual the other political (though the lines of demarcation are hardly clear), lived and moved was consistently counterpoised to the established church and its mores, on the one hand, and to the established sociopolitical order with its connotations of colour, on the other. Both men had large followings of aggressively black, lower-class, "downpressed" Jamaicans. It is within this same psychological environment, this same population, that the Rastafarian faith found believers, whether they functioned as part of an organized group or as "own-built", i.e. Rastas following the philosophy on an individual level and not attached to any particular group. The physical link between the Rastafari and their heroes may have been "obscure" as Smith et al. (1960) suggest,[5] but the ideological similarities are unmistakable. On the prophetic level, Bedward is said to have foretold the coming of Haile Selassie and there are those of his followers who feel that the coincidence of his death with the crowning of Haile Selassie is not insignificant.[6]

Some comments from the literature on the socioeconomic milieu of the movement are to the point. The earliest researcher into the Rastafarian belief system was G.E. Simpson of Oberlin College, Ohio, who, under the sponsorship

---

4 Bedward, *Daily Gleaner*, January 1895. This report verbatim from the *Daily Gleaner* (in Elkins 1977) differs from the report verbatim from the *Post* (in Chevannes 1971). It is likely that both represent approximations to Bedward's speech as reported by English officials.

5 Subsequent research suggests that the link was not really obscure. Howell, one of the earliest exponents of Rastafarian theology (Haile Selassie as God), is said to have appealed to those of the Garveyites who where "poorest and most exploited" as opposed to the "better-off black" and "lower status brown" ones (Post 1970). Robert Hinds, Howell's chief assistant, is said to have been a Bedwardite.

6 The implication is that Bedward could die in peace in November 1930 because Haile Selassie was crowned then; the black Saviour of the world had come (interview with Roman Henry, March 1979).

of the Institute of Social and Economic Research of the then University College of the West Indies, carried out research in 1953. His is a sociological work and he places the members of the Rastafarian groups at the lowest socioeconomic levels of the society:

> Cult members, some of whom have arrived only recently from country districts and many of whom are unemployed or underemployed, live in crowded one- or two-room houses. The men who are employed are engaged in low-paid unskilled or semi-skilled work. Women of the area find employment as domestic servants, street merchants and shop-keepers. Those who are not fully employed "scuffle" for a living. This expressive term means doing odd jobs, running errands, selling firewood, making baskets or other craft products ... in short, doing almost anything that enables one to keep alive.
> (Simpson 1970, 203)

He describes the attitude of the Jamaican middle class to the Rastafarian brethren as one of "contempt and disgust" (219). Seven years later a three-man team from the University of the West Indies undertook a historical study, noting under "work", a subheading of "The Doctrines of the Movement", that "much of the psychology of the brethren is the psychology of the unemployed in any place of the world ... The movement is rooted in unemployment" (Smith et al. 1960, 28). Additional implications appear in the section "The Movement's Current Organization": "In the dense slum areas the prevailing doctrine and ideology is now Ras Tafari: in the equally dense and better-built lower-income areas such as Jones Town, Rose Town, Admiral Town, Trench and Denham Town, the doctrine is well represented" (30).

Their comment on the attitudes of people even very little better off is implied: "Occasionally one finds a family, some members of which are Rastafari living in a concrete bungalow. More commonly when young men show Ras Tafari behaviours, their parents react sharply and the young man leaves home in disgrace" (30).

The early history of the Ras Tafari movement, then, is rooted in the cultures of revival, politics, and poverty. We shall see how inextricably these are bound up with protest and protest with language.

Rastafari Protest

It has been observed, in discussing the Christian religion, that the Ten Commandments were not given because of a whim of the Almighty but were offered in response to certain misdemeanours to which the Israelites had become prone. Similarly it can be said that the Rastafarian belief system, while it may indeed be a twentieth-century revelation, must also be seen as a philosophy in response to the Jamaican situation and to all that the establishment has represented historically for the sons of slaves growing up in what a recent researcher labels a "pigmentocracy" in which "blackness became equated with lowliness and servility, whiteness with power and godliness" (Albuquerque 1977, 136). The acceptance of a black monarch must be seen against the rejection of the traditional English monarchy (particularly the Queens Elizabeth I and II, who are said to be whores); the acceptance of an African heaven on earth (Ethiopia), whose black God is the king, against the Christian paradise in the sky where a white God reigns with white angels (the Pope as the white devil in Revelations on the sacred side, and the head of the Mafia on the secular side fall somewhere within this response); the "natural" physical image of unshaved head and face, and in the case of woman the unadorned body, against the local established ideal of clean-shaven man and painted woman; and the forceful creative turn of words against English, the language used by the oppressor to "increase confusion".

Researchers in the social sciences tend to require a framework, a model into which to fit phenomena they study. As a result, the Rastafarian community has been described as a "political cult" (Simpson 1955), a "messianic movement" (Barrett 1968), a "millenarian movement" (Albuquerque 1977), and a "politico-religious protest cult" (Kitzinger 1969), among other labels.[7] But as the researchers move into the details of their descriptions, all present in one form or another the content of "protest" in the belief system of the movement.

It is to the social history of Jamaica, however, that one must look to understand the depth and the breadth of the protest that the Rastafarian belief system represents and of which the Rastafari, in all his complexity, is a symbol. The Rastafarian Movement is what Nettleford (1978), refining his own earlier definition (in Owens 1976), describes as one of Plantation America's "most authentic expressions of *organic* revolt in appropriate if anguished response to some of the deepest social forces that have shaped and still determine the discrepancies of our Caribbean society" (188, my emphasis). The operative terms here are surely "revolt" and "organic". Lanternari (1963), looking briefly at Rastafarianism as one religion of the oppressed, describes it as a "typically escapist movement rather than a revolutionary force" (163). His definition of revolution differs significantly from Nettleford's and, as we shall see, the revolution is on, although it might not be taking traditional and expected forms. The key is

---

7 Yawney (1976) admits that "Rastafarianism is a complex phenomenon which cannot be analysed easily in terms of strictly traditional models of utopian or millenarian movements ... In Jamaica ... Rastafarianism takes on the added dimension of a popular front in a cultural and symbolic sense" (232).

"organic", which suggests that what was/is happening is moving in the only way that it can if it springs from the soil of this Jamaica of which the social historians are aware.

Nettleford (1978), quoting Theodor Adorno, puts this chapter's interest in the revolution in perspective: "Social protest manifests itself in language change. For defiance of society includes defiance of its language" (18, n. 29), and defends the Rastafari's implied reaction of "the impulsive semantic urge simply to call old social categories by new and fashionable borrowings" and the creation of a "battery of 'I-words' " as part of their "small but pointedly relevant lexicon of normative-descriptive word-symbols" (201).

Dread Talk

In the first chapter of this book I describe Dread Talk (DT) as an example of "lexical expansion within a creole system" (in this case Jamaica Creole [JC]) where the lexicon changes to reflect the philosophical position of the speaker. I set up three categories within which to examine the lexicon of DT:

Category I   In which known items bear new meanings, e.g. chalice = pipe for smoking ganja

Category II   In which words bear the weight of their phonological implications, e.g. "downpress" for oppress

Category III   /ai/ words
i. Pronominal function, e.g. I, I-man (I; me)
ii. Initial syllable[8] replacement, e.g. I-la-lu (callaloo)

---

8 Initial syllable is the more accurate term for what I called "initial consonant" in 1979.

It will be necessary to make reference to these categories as we look at the history of Dread Talk.

Chevannes (1979) attributes to the Youth Black Faith, a Rastafarian camp of young men who came together about 1949, the "jargon presently attributed to the Rastafari as a whole" (189). While this group may indeed have initiated DT, it is also possible that the same phenomenon appeared in different Rasta camps in different degrees over a period of time. Let us look at some reactions in the literature on Rastafari.

The fact that Simpson (1955) does not isolate it for special attention and that Smith et al. (1960) mention it only as part of a point on violence[9] need not indicate an absence of Dread Talk in the speech of the early Rastafari with whom they came in contact. What is included in any study depends on the focus of the researcher. Besides, not all Rastas use the language (though most use at least the Category III words); those who do, do not use it at all times and, perhaps most important, the Rastafari code-switch with the same facility as other Jamaica Creole speakers. Barrett (1977), who seemed to ignore it in his early research, in his later research takes DT into account and comments:

> it is a religious language of a strange type. Few outsiders can make sense of what the average cultist says. In the first place it is ungrammatical when spoken by the uneducated, secondly it is Jamaican dialect used on the philosophic level, a burden which it was not created to bear;[10] and finally the Rastafarian

---

9 "The language of the movement is violent. This is because it is the language of the Bible, and especially of the Old Testament. It is apocalyptic language, in which sinners are consumed with fire; sheep are separated from goats, oppressors are smitten and kings and empires are overthrown" (27).

10 In rebuttal of this point by Barrett consider Rohlehr's (1971) article, specifically his explication of the lyrics of the song "Bongo Nyah".

speech is almost devoid of subject-object opposition as well as without verbs. Students of Rastafarianism must be prepared to translate the material into English, or to do research only among the most educated brethren. (143)

Most of Barrett's comments could equally have been made about JC itself. What is reinforced here is the fact that the researchers can hardly help us in terms of the timing of the appearance of DT as it is known today and while Chevannes (1979) suggests a time for its appearance we know nothing about how general its use became and how soon. It is only when we come to the sixties that there is concrete evidence for such discussion. In talking about the language of the Rastafari in the fifties Chevannes (1979) is careful to quote Martha Beckwith's remark concerning the facility with which Jamaicans pun – what she calls the "easy loquacity" of the Jamaican peasant – and he sees the Youth Black Faith's linguistic input as merely "carrying the tradition further" (189). While this remark becomes important when we look at the spread of DT outside the Rastafarian community, it relates only to Category II of DT words. This might lead us to suggest that this was the only feature (apart from the violent Biblical language) that emerged in the fifties. It could of course be that Chevannes, a sociologist, was speaking as loosely as Barrett does in the quotation above. He also suffered the disadvantage of having to reconstruct information about the fifties from oral sources collected in the seventies.

The feature that most identifies Dread Talk today, however, is neither the Biblical turn of phrase nor the punning per se but the "I-ance", what Nettleford (1978) calls the "battery of 'I-words'" (my Category III). The next in order is what he describes as the "small but pointedly relevant lexicon of normative descriptive word-symbols" (my Categories I and II). It is in these categories that the stance of protest, of revolt in words, is evident. Yawney (1972), commenting on the importance of these creative words, says: "To the Rastas, words are seals of the mind, words have power and they must not be abused but rather used with awareness" (30).[11] She gives this rationale for DT: "The Rastas have always resented English as the language of colonialism and have developed their own [language] based on its bastardization" (32).

Her terminology, however, betrays her vantage point. For the Rastafari himself sees his "doctoring" of the language in quite a different light. Chevannes' Youth Black Faith informant sees it as "stepping up" the language and Bongo Jerry (1970) sees it as taking the unfortunate "double meaning" out of English, which he describes as "crossword speaking … word rearranging/ringing rings of roses, pocket full of poses" (15). "Double meaning" here is perhaps a bit of a misnomer for what is conceived of as a kind of inaccuracy on the phonological level (as in OPpress for an activity that is in fact DOWNpressing).

Double meaning is in fact a term that could be used to describe the punning of which Beckwith spoke and to which Chevannes makes reference. It forms the most hilarious, though not the most protesting, category of DT word usage. Observe how it works with Category III in the following comment by a Rasta spokesman in which he compares the lack of awareness of Babylon (the establishment) with the

---

11 Note in this connection that Brathwaite (1974) sees the emphasis on the word and its importance as an African survival in the creole context/complex. He writes: "The process of transformation … has its roots in a certain kind of concern for and attitude to the word, the atomic core of language. This is something that is very much present in all folk cultures, at pre-literate, pre-industrial societies. Within such cultures, language was and is a creative act in itself. Think of our love for the politician or the word of the preacher" (90). See also his "Nametracks" from *Mother Poem* (1977). Note that the Rastafari sees himself as a particularly African brother.

awareness of the Rasta man: "But eyes have they and see not, only Fari could see …" (Rastafari Movement Association [RMA] 1976, 3).[12]

Perhaps a comment on the importance of "seeing" as understanding in the DT usage is to the point here. Yawney (1972), underlining the fact that "great significance is attached to seeing", comments that "SEE" appears at the beginning and the end of Selassie's name because he is the beginning and the end (note that he is also frequently referred to as Alpha and Omega) and that "Selassie I" becomes "Selassie *eye*". It is hardly coincidental that the rejoinder to indicate understanding of any matter is /siin/ "seen". So that the Rasta man "reasoning" with a group will frequently interrupt himself with this interjection, and his listeners, on the other hand, are allowed to use the same sound to mean "yes I understand". The following extract from a session of reasoning should illustrate that feature as well as some of the others mentioned earlier:

> you nuo av silasi ai/ you nuo av im/ you nuo av im/
> (who?)
> av silasi ai/ sista we aks di kwestyan/
> (well I …)
> nuo/ nuo a miin/ mii/ ai baan aa gruo iina jamieka/ luk ier
> no/ ai baan aa gruo iina jamieka/ which iz rofli nain hondred
> an ad mailz ferda fram afrika/ ferda fram itiopya/
> (no, no I know about Selassie …)
> luk/ luk ier/ a nat ofendid bai/ fers ting a waa yu nuo/ se a
> nat ofendid bai di riiznin/ dat iz di fers ting/ so yu kyan jos
> kuul/ siin/ wel wat a waa aks yu nou/ yu nuo moch av im/
> (well no)
> wel iz wa/ yu nuo iz riili bad/ far az a blak persn nou/ yu av

---

12 Understand "far (seeing) eye" – pun on "fari".

sertn piipl/ nat iivn az a blak persn/ as a sitizn av dis werl/ far
ai nuo se dem piipl ier nuo a sobstanshal amount about
empara iel silasi fers/ yu no siit/jos bikaa dem piipl si tu it se
dem nuo waa gwaan fina ert/
(Bongo Jerry 1969)

Do you know of Selassi I? Do you know of him? Do you
know of him?
(Well I ... I ...)
Of Selassi I, the sister who asked the question.
(Who?)
No, no I mean, me, I was born and grew up in Jamaica. Look
here. I was born and grew up in Jamaica which is roughly
nine hundred and more miles away from Africa, away from
Ethiopia.
(No, no, no, I know about Selassi ...)
Look, look here, I am not offended by ... first thing I want
you to know, that I am not offended by the reasoning; that is
the first thing. So you can just be cool. Seen? Well what I
want to ask you now, do you know much of him?
(Well no)
Well it's what ... you know ... that is really bad for as a black
person now ... you have certain people not even as a black
person, as a citizen of this world ... for I know that these people here know a substantial amount about Emperor Haile
Selassi first; don't you see? Just because these people see to it
that they know what is going on the world.

This is an excerpt from a reasoning of the late sixties after the
word of Rastafari had started its spread through the music which
was expressive of much that was happening in the society then.

The Sixties – Protest Music and Language

The sixties were turbulent and confusing times in Jamaica[13] as depressed economic conditions, burgeoning urban unemployment, and reverberations of the Black Power movement in the USA converged. An important reflection of the pressure of the times was the music that emerged from the depressed areas, a compound of traditional Jamaican folk music, American pop, and Rastafari drums. Gordon Rohlehr (1969) writing of this period says that the musicians "effected a transformation of a variety of external and local music into a particularly Jamaican sound" and comments, "I believe that this transformation was partly due to the increasing pressure of life in Kingston during the sixties and the musician's increasing awareness of these pressures."

This musical explosion cannot be overemphasized since the music became the one element common to all parts of a society of "almost obscene economic extremes" and of strikingly contrasting philosophical poses. In what seemed like the twinkling of an eye all classes of Jamaica were moving to music that had been reserved for lower-class dance halls, and drawing-rooms resounded with a beat that shouted for loin movement to tunes from which parents had protected their children's ears a decade earlier. The music was in protest of the establishment but the establishment was accepting the music. Such was the paradox of the overwhelming Jamaican acceptance of the Ska, later of the Rock Steady and finally of the Reggae. Such was to be their overwhelming internalization of the language of the lyrics that were developing. In the Jamaica of the late twenties, the lines of demarcation between Garvey's political protest and Bedward's revivalist protest were by no means clear. In the Jamaica of the sixties the lines between violent youth protest

---

13 For a detailed commentary on the political and literary ferment at the time see Brathwaite 1977b.

(represented by the "Rudies" or "Rude Boys")[14] against the system and poor economic conditions, Black Power protest and Rastafarian protest were equally blurred. Kitzinger (1969), researching at that time, described the Rastafari as being "in opposition to whatever Jamaica Government happen(ed) to be in power" (27). An excerpt from a Black Power speech of the time could, with a few linguistic changes, easily have been made by a Rastafarian spokesman:

> Whites have dominated us both mentally and physically …
> The most profound revelation of the sickness of the question of race is our respect for all the white symbols. (Rodney 1969, 31–2)

Compare it with an excerpt from a Rastafarian speech of a later date:

> Jamaica indulges in an inferior complex – a pretentious class system, so it becomes a hypocritical, segregated society.
> (RMA 1969)

What I am suggesting here is that the common political anguish belonged to a whole cross-section of the society, exclusive of its religious or philosophical affiliation/non-affiliation. Common musical forms sprang up out of the protest against the economic and political situation: "The compositions of ska and its offsprings, the rock steady and reggae, were to serve as a common mode of artistic expression among a wide cross section of the youth of Jamaica" (Nettleford 1970, 98).

The language of the Rastafari, which was/is in fact Jamaica Creole "stepped up" to accommodate certain philosophical positions, was *ready and in place as a vehicle to convey the*

---

14 For comments on this phenomenon see Nettleford 1970 and White 1967.

urgent message of protest.[15] Chevannes' comment on the natural way in which the Jamaican peasant language accommodates puns must be repeated here to emphasize how easily the Rastafarian speech was adapted, though not merely in its punning propensity, as a means of expressing deep anti-establishment feelings, no matter from whose lips. The "Rude Boy", anxious to describe the unfairness of the system of justice/injustice, could write a tune called "Judge Dread" using a very significant item of the Rastafarian lexicon.[16] A popular singer wanting to record what Rohlehr (1969) speaks of as "the common man's growing frustration with his lot" could wail "Poor me Israelites".[17] There were, as well, songs predicting large-scale political catastrophe: "Look ya now Pharaoh house crash", "Babylon Burnin", "What a Fire". While Pharaoh is not recognizable as a popular Rastafarian butt, Babylon certainly is and the Fire is part of the same apocalyptic language that researchers picked up as part of an aura of violence. As the sixties gave way to the seventies, Reggae took over as *the* popular music form – and Reggae has employed, almost exclusively, the language of Rastafari. Count Ossie (of blessed memory) in an interview in the early seventies speaking of the role of Rasta said "We were fighting colonialism and oppression but not with gun and bayonet, but wordically, culturally" (*Swing* Sept./Oct. 1972). Perhaps this is the "organic" revolt of which Nettleford (1978) speaks.

---

15 I believe that Rohlehr saw this but took it to be chiefly a phenomenon within one man, Don Drummond the genius trombonist of the early sixties. See his "Sounds and Pressure" (1969), for example.

16 Chevannes (1979) sees the early concept of Dread as almost synonymous with "mystic"; Owens' book (1976) illustrates the word in its variety of latter-day meanings.

17 Rohlehr (1969) sees this as an implied comparison with the experience of the Jews, "a comparison common among blacks". But in the Jamaican context, where the Rastafari have identified themselves as the "true" Israelites, I would think that the choice of term reflects Rastafari influence rather than any more general view.

The Seventies – Reggae Music and Message

Count Ossie's statement becomes more meaningful if we understand the place that the message takes in the Rastafarian scheme of things. One spokesman describes it in this way: "The Rastafarian shamanizes his cultural values in music and Arts and confounds the Reggaematics which is a message from and to the King, as it is written Sing unto God praises of His name" (RMA 1976, 3).

Another spokesman from a different group comments not only on the place of music but on the lack of awareness of Babylon who hears it:

> kaa you nuo/ aal i muzik pan i rieydyo we riili a se eniting a
> rasta/ a jos muuzik tu dem/ sed ting ya/ you no siit/
> (Bongo Jerry 1969)

> Because all the music on the radio that is really saying
> anything is Rasta music. It is just music to them (Babylon),
> that's the thing don't you see?

A foreign popular commentator sees the reggae musicians as "Jamaica's prophets, social commentators and shamans" (Davis and Simon 1977). Brodber and Greene (1979), sociologist and political scientist, discussing the song "as a communicative device" explain that one of the characteristics of the theocratic world government, which all Rastafarian sects see as the next phase of social and political evolution, is that the "singers as well as the players of instruments shall be there" (Psalm 87, v. 7) and comment, "There is divine sanction therefore for the existence of singers and other musicians. The Rastafarian singers accordingly view their role as a social and religious responsibility" (13).

But to understand the impact of the song on the non-

Rastafarian public that receives it, it is necessary to appreciate the place of popular music in the Jamaican society. Mention has already been made of the enthusiastic reception of the musical explosion of the sixties. Brodber and Greene (1979) put the reaction in a wider perspective when they see Jamaican society as an example of a diaspora society and comment on the response to music common among such people: "Dispersed Africans given similar conditions in the New World, and given as well the new and urgent need to communicate from day to day in public places without being understood by the enemy, continued to use this form of communication" (2). They quote the words of a fictional diaspora man, Manuel, in Jacques Romain's *Masters of the Dew*: "I enjoyed myself like a real negro. When the drum beats, I feel it in the pit of my stomach. I feel an itch in my loins and an electric current in my legs, and I've got to join the dance." And perhaps Ras Daniel Hartman (1972) speaks not only for Rastafari but for all Jamaica when he puts it succinctly thus: "Music is I, and I am music, for man is music and music alone shall live through man."

So the fanatical response of the Jamaican public, specifically Jamaican youth to each new disc that hits the market and the disproportionate popularity of the disc jockey (DJ) is perhaps part of an inheritance. The music is heard constantly on the corner or coming over the hills from the sound systems and it is heard at home on the expensive stereophonic sets of middle- and high-income families. "The words of the singers have penetrated the class barrier through the disc" ,comment Brodber and Greene (1979) whose concern is for the message of the word and its possible impact on the hearers. Our own concern is for the word itself.

Dread Talk – The Language of Youth

We have seen how the sons of Babylon have come to hear the word not merely from the Rasta man in the streets but from message-bearers coming in on the airwaves in their homes. It is in this way, I think, that the language has come to be separated from the burden of the message it bears. For Dread Talk today is no longer exclusively speech representing a certain sect/ion of the Jamaican society, a certain philosophy within the society. It has become a general way of speaking. Today DT is used for identifying one youth man with another. Albuquerque, commenting on the Rastafarian movement in general and on language in particular, says, "clearly the movement's contributions to Jamaican society were/are remarkable. The net effect has been Rastafarianization of Jamaica and while certain phrases and expressions have evolved from Rasta youth, their distribution in the general population is widespread" (302).

The language no longer (necessarily) connotes commitment to the problems of the "sufferer" or to Rastafari. The language no longer walks hand in hand with the beard, the short drop strut and the sometimes visionary eyes of the traditional Rasta man. The middle-class parent who yesteryear sweated and prayed lest yet another son might be "turning Rasta" when his language suggests it, protests now on aesthetic and pseudo-educational grounds, or frequently does not bat an eyelid when his son answers the telephone not with the traditional falsetto "Hi!" but with the low drum /airi/ I-ri! a mere comma after conversing with him in Standard Jamaican English.

And Rasta has become the unit of Jamaican man. In the talk of the young people, "Yes Rasta" is frequently heard where "Yes man" was used before. And everywhere, for assent or merely as an indication of attention, one hears /siin/ "seen" or /siin aiya/ "seen I-yah".

It remains for me to illustrate how Dread Talk functions within the Jamaica Talk of some young people in our society. We shall examine excerpts from samples of schoolboy discussions and I will present a list of "new" Jamaican words and expressions put together by a group of young people in an English language workshop.[18] The excerpts are from recordings of in-class discussions taped in a sixth form (Grade 13) class in a Jamaican high school for boys. The Rastafari movement is very strongly male oriented (Owens 1976). It is understandable, therefore, that the linguistic influence is most pronounced in the speech of young men. The boys whose speech is recorded here represent "educated" youth and, given the democratization of the Jamaican educational system in the late fifties, should represent at least the middle and lower socioeconomic levels of our society (though the reality is that the very poor hardly reach high school and when they do, rarely reach the sixth form). The in-class situation is chosen to illustrate the extent to which Dread Talk, particularly a few key expressions, has penetrated even the formal situation that is the classroom, in this case the General English Paper preparation class. (This discussion is about Rastafarianism.)

I(a) briekin fram di oul plaantieshan sistim/ di rastafieran a di fers man dat staat gyaadn plaantin/ rait nou dem se bwai dem naa dipen paa no man/ dem naa dipen paa no big man fi get chruu/ dem jos a do a likl aam/ selfrilians yu nuo/ dem a go plaant op vegitebl/ ailalu an aal den ting de ...	breaking from the old plantation system the Rastafarian is the first man that start(ed) garden planting right now they say boy they are not depending on any man, not depending on any big man to get through; they are just doing a little self-reliance you know, they are going to plant up vegetables, callaloo and all those things ...

18 Thanks are due to Mrs Kathryn Shields for permission to use her tapes and to Miss Olive Senior who kindly offered reading material including the list here mentioned. Thanks also to the members of Miss Senior's group who compiled the list.

(b) lisn mi nou mis/about dis huol/ ruul an ring dem a taak bout/ bai dem nuo se/ bai bai wierbai rasta man liv/ bot mis/ ai a wanda/ simpl/ di biesik ting wid dem rasta man tingz is lov/ siin/ so dat ef yu jos liv mis/ wid lov az yu gaidlain/ a duo si ou/ yu duo riili niid no riili ruul an ting/ ... tek di simpl kansep av lov mis/ yu riili si ow sertn tingz mos bi rang/ laik waar/ envyos an den ting de/ no mos bi rang/ yu no siit

Listen to me now Miss, about this whole rule and thing they are talking about. Because they know that by, by, whereby Rasta man live but Miss, I am wondering, simply, the basic thing with those Rasta men's things is love; see? So that if you just live Miss, with love as your guideline, I don't see how ... you don't really need any really rule and thing ... take the simple concept of love Miss, you really see how certain things must be wrong; like war, envious (envy?) and things like those must be wrong.

Discussion

I have written elsewhere (see chapter 1) on the extent to which Dread Talk is Jamaica Creole with certain adjustments. On the phonological level I have singled out the /a/ which is the counterpart of the English /ɔ/ sound and which, noticeable in JC, is exaggerated in DT, as if this symbol of true creole must be stressed and must be perfected for identification. It is this sound that alters the Rastafarian reading of a chapter of the Bible to such an extent that the casual listener is not sure he is in fact hearing the accustomed words. This is the vowel in words like /fram/ and /plantieshan/ from excerpt I(a).

On the lexical level in this same excerpt note that /ailalu/ is preferred to the creole /kalalu/ observing the initial syllable replacement with /ai/ of my Category II words. In excerpt I(b) this /ai/ occurs in its pronominal function where it is regularly substituted for the JC /mi/ as in /ai a wanda/. Of course it could be argued here that this is an instance of the English first person subject pronoun. But if this had been the case one would expect the auxiliary form "am" + "ing", thus a possible "I am wondering". I am suggesting that the /ai/ used here is the DT form that alternates with /aiman/ and /aianai/. Note in this excerpt the use of /siin/ and /yu no siit/, alternate forms of the rhetorical device which in DT is more than a space filler since the idea of *seeing* is so important. Consider an exchange between the class teacher and a pupil, recorded at the end of the discussion of which these two excerpts are fragments:

> Teacher: I want to comment on the language ... you are not conscious of it. You are not conscious of the words; how many were/are in the Jamaican language which are English and how many are Rasta language. You will find that more than fifty percent of your speech is Rasta language. I was just thinking of our education and how we are going to extricate or release ourselves from that – er – language.
> Pupil: So why we have to release ourself from it Miss?
> Teacher: Because we are writing an exam that is also foreign.

Excerpts II(a) and (b) which follow were taped a week after that exchange: (This discussion is about a forthcoming political demonstration.)

II(a) now mai viuz an di ting dier mis/ di demanstrieshan/ fers ting/ ai am simpatetik tu di demanstrieshan/ bot ai am nat far it bikaa you si/ wen you luk an it mis/ a duon si ow riili an chuuli piipl benifit fram it/

Now my views on the thing there Miss, the demonstration; first thing I am sympathetic to the demonstration but I am not for it because you see when you look on it Miss, I don't see how really and truly people benefit from it.

Teacher: wiet wiet/ clarifai somthing agen/ a duon onderstan/ you ar simpathetik bot you not for it/

Teacher: Wait, wait. Clarify something again; I don't understand. You are sympathetic but you are not for it?

Yie mis/ a miin di riizn far di demanstrieshan/ a miin wel di praisiz kaina hai an riili an chuuli dred/ *siin*/ an dem waa fi mek it nuon se wel raitnow bwai it dred aa wi kyaa riili bier it/ bot a miin di demanstrieshan we dem waant/ bai klouzin shap aa piipl nat going to werk/ a kyaa agri wid it/

Yes Miss. I mean the reason for the demonstration; I mean well the prices are kind of high and really and truly dread; seen? and they want to make it known that well right now boy it dread and we can't really bear it. But the demonstration that they want by closing shop and people not going to work, I can't agree with it.

II(b) ... dis prais inkries/ iz/ fa dat riizn/ ... rait/ laik tek kaan biif dala nainti trii/ bap/ gaan skai hai/ man kudn afuod/ aam/ fi bai rais an ting/ you no *siit*/ aa yuuz im bred an im kaan biif/ you si dat gaan outa im riich nou/ so im afi kaina

this price increase is, for that reason ... right ... like take corned beef a dollar ninety-three bap! gone sky high. Man couldn't afford ... to buy rice and thing, don't you see? and use his bread and his corned beef you see that is gone out of his

tink a sopm/ a sopm els/ flowa gaan op tu/ so im afi tink a kasaada an aal den ting de/ so iz stil a huol heepa/ a miin/ planin fi di likl man/ *sait*/ an i stil afek di skuul chiljren an di huol/

reach now so he has to think of something else ... something else ... flour gone up too so he has to think of cassava and all those things so it's still a whole heap of I mean planning for the little man. Sight. And it still affects the school children on the whole ...

Judging from this sample, the class teacher's estimate of fifty percent of the words being DT is a wild overstatement of the case. Indeed the examples of lexical items that are from DT can be singled out in II(a) as the use of the word "dread" in two different ways and of the interjection "seen" once. In II(b) there are "seen" and its alternate, "sight", and the form "man" unmarked by an article. It is, however, the overall effect that prevents her from analysing accurately what is happening. When the /a/ is frequent and "seen" is interjected there is no need for much else to identify speech as DT. In fact, it is true to say that any one trait of DT can throw language over the border from JC to DT. This happens frequently with the use of the "I-words" so dreaded by those who consider Rasta anathema.

One might question the absence of the well used "I-man" from the excerpts presented here but these are taken from discussions which are to some extent formal. An aside in the same class in which excerpts I(a) and I(b) were taped runs:

aiman nuo wai you laaf/ di brejrin de ...	I know why you laugh; the fellow there ...

and an informal exchange between boys in another group at the same academic level goes:

1st boy: yes man/ widout lov[19] bad/ aiman wuda bai it/	2nd boy: yes rasta

I commented earlier, but only in passing, on the low tonal level of DT, as in the greetings /aits/ and /airi/. I have found, however, that while speech recorded among the Rastafari indicates the ability to maintain this tone over long periods, the schoolboy samples do not reflect it to the same extent, whether because they are unable to maintain it or because they see it as less important to the image of identity than the other traits is hard to tell.

The notion that Dread Talk and Jamaica Talk are hardly distinguishable is a threatening notion to those who are suspicious of what Rastafari means in the Jamaican context. But in actual usage among the young, one is slowly being "colonized" by the other. Below are words extracted from a list of "new" Jamaican words and expressions put together by a group of employees at one of our local radio stations in an English language workshop. It is titled a "Preliminary List of 'Jamaicanisms' in Use since the Publication of Cassidy and

---

19 A popular record.

LePage *Dictionary of Jamaican English*". Of the 307 words and expressions listed, 148 are recognizable from the lexicon of DT.[20] I have retained the glosses given by the compilers but I have placed these words into categories in terms of my Categories I, II and III and have added a Category IV to accommodate those words that I consider genuine "creations" in that they have been applied to phenomena with little reverence for (or reference to) the English or Creole meanings of the root words.

Category I

In which known items bear new meanings

Arnold	pork
Babylon	police; policeman; soldier or people who are called wicked by the Rastafari; place of wickedness; oppressors; to do with an unprincipled way of life usually in reference to the white man's culture
bald head	person not dealing with Rasta; non-believer of the dread culture; person who has not got his hair in locks; person who does not believe in Rastafarian religion
blessings	salutations
bredda (a, or one)	a boy
bredren	male friend(s) holding same beliefs as the speaker
bun (weed)	smoke (ganja)

---

20 This recognition is purely subjective and depends entirely on my own acquaintance with the lexicon of DT.

chalice[21]	chillum pipe (for smoking marijuana)
check	see; look for; visit; to befriend the opposite sex
colly; colly weed	ganja (marijuana)
control	keep; take; look after
cool	alright; at ease
dally	ride; cycle; erratic movements done while riding bike; to ride zigzag on a bike or bicycle; manoeuvre on motor-cycle ridden mainly by ghetto youth
dat	pork
dawta; daughta	girlfriend; girl; woman; female companion; wife; name given to any young woman
dis man	me
dread	true Rasta man; Rasta; one who believes in Rasta religion; bad, ter-rible
dread!	Hail! — a greeting
dread locks	Rasta
dread nut	coconut
dub	good piece of Reggae instrumental; flip side of Reggae 45; musical ver-sion of song usually with few or no lyrics; a rhythmic and visceral beat played mainly with drums, bass guitar, and one or two percussion instruments

---

21 The question "What is a chalice?" posed to a group of upper-school teenagers received answers like "a pipe", "a kind of pipe?" until one, seeing the anxiety on an attending adult's face, admitted "it is a thing in the church".

feel it	great pain; hardship or death
first day	yesterday
first night	last night
folly	joking
forward	move; go; leave
forward step	make a move
give thanks	an expression of gratitude for life or some kind of gesture
go deh	continue; move along; phrase of approval advising continuation like "right on"
gorgon	king, bully, a person who is tops in what he does; toughest; best; ruthless person
grounds	sociable
guidance	May God (Jah) go with you
hail	greetings; salutation on meeting or saying goodbye
herb	marijuana
jester; jestering	kidding; joking, playing around; not sincere, not acting right
lick (weed; a cup; the chalice)	smoke (ganja; chillum pipe)
locks	the strands of a Rasta's hair
love; one love	a greeting
lock down	arrest
megry	business turned sour
moap	soap
more time	later; see you

morgue	refrigerator
natty	a person with locks; a Rastafari; unkempt hair; dreadlocks (Rasta)
penetrate	admire; search for truth
queen	Rasta's wife or sweetheart, wife or girlfriend; a man's female companion (commonly used in Rastafarian circles)
ranking; top ranking	person who is OK
higher ranking	above average
high ranking	a leader
reason	discuss; talk
red	high on ganja or drugs; angry
rest	leave off
rockers	lively reggae music; local music with heavy rhythm; hard driving reggae rhythm; new name for reggae
roots	from the earth; down to earth; original; a greeting
running(s)	happenings
seat up	take a seat
seen; seen? seen!	understand; understanding; to comprehend or overstand; understand? yes!
sight; sight up	understood; understand
skate	bike; motorbike (I man a step on I skate – I am about to leave i.e. ride my bike)

skeef	girl, woman (I man would bite of that skeef – I would make love to that girl)
sound: block a	speak
spit a	speak
seal up the	to complete
spar	friend; platonic friend
star	guys; men
step	leave; move on
step it	to leave; go away
step inna earth	make a move
stepper	gunman
strictly	only
structure	the human body
struggle with a structure	make love to a girl
sufferer	poor; ghetto liver[22]
tribalist	troublesome
trod	leave; walk away
version	instrumental side of reggae record
weed	ganja
weed of wisdom	ganja
wooden suit	coffin

---

22 Note that "liver" in Jamaica Creole can mean "one who lives".

Category II

In which words bear the weight of their phonological implications

downpression	depression
down press	depress
higherstand	understand
Jah-man-can	Jamaican
Jamdown; Jamdung	Jamaica
outformer	police informer
upfull	righteous (author's gloss)

Category III

I words and Y words

I aan ya	I am here
I an I a knacka	my heart is good
I n I; I an I	me; I; we; mine, myself
I-bage; ibbage	cabbage
I-ceive	receive
I-cient	ancient
I-ah; iya	me
ichin	ganja
I-ditate	meditate
idren, idren, idren	my friend, male or female friend holding same beliefs as speaker; colleague brother (friend)
I-dure	endure
I-fant	infant

I-ficially	officially
I-hold	behold
I-kril	mackerel
I-laloo	callaloo
I-ly; ile; iley; highly	ganja
I-men	amen
I-matis	tomato
imes	times
inago	mango
inana; inanna	banana
inderstand	understand
iney; inie; inney	greetings; nice; pleasing; good
inite	unite
I-nointed	anointed
I-nually	annually; continually
I-polin	dumpling
in the strong	next week
ipa	pepper
I-quality	equality
I-rate	create
I-ration	creation
irie; irey; ire	alright; good; appreciation of; pleasing; a salutation
irie skip	yes, friend
I-rits	spirits
irons	gun

iron bird	airplane
iron fish	ship
I-rous	desirous
I-sanna	Hosanna
I-serve	deserve (author's gloss)
I-ses	praises
I-schence	incense; ganja
I-sire	desire
I-smit	transmit
I-ssembly	assembly
ital; I-tal; itol	vital; pure natural; organic; food cooked without salt; Rasta food
I-talise	vitalize
ital bath	river bath
yanks	thanks
yata	girl or young miss
yife	life
yocho	chocho (green vegetable)
yook	stick (jook [a prick, as in pin prick])
yountry	country
yudd; yude; yudde	food

(The reason for hyphenation of some "I-words" and not others is not clear.)

Category IV

New Items

Atops	Red Stripe Beer
backative	stamina; strength
bongoniah (Bungo Niah)	a Rasta
deaders; deadahs; deddas	meat
dunny; dunney; dunza	money
freenana	banana
sata; satta	relax; stay where you are; keep calm; stay on; stay put; rest; quiet
spliff	ganja

Discussion

While these lists are not presented as a complete lexicon of Rastafari words or even of Dread Talk words in Jamaica Creole, certain tendencies emerge that are worthy of comment. Lists in Categories I and III are long compared with those in Categories II and IV. I believe that this discrepancy is not the result of the non-Rastafari nature of the compilers (and therefore implied ignorance) but does in fact represent the proportions not only in DT as used by the Rastafari but in DT as it has been captured by the wider community. Words in Category II are obviously easy to create. That list is therefore potentially the longest and the frequency of the occurrence of these words in any speech act will depend on the commitment of the speaker to the style of speech.

On the level of meaning, it is worthy of note that several of the words, which are recognizable but now bear different meanings (Category I), have to do with music and with the smoking of ganja, two activities in which the society regards the Rasta man as the major participant. It is in these areas where he functions most that he must most make/re-make words. And among the coinages, note how the Rastafarian way of life affects the choice of term assigned to articles. The man who can label "meat" DEADahs, is hardly a man who eats it. The serious Rastafari rejects meat and eats only I-tal food, which consists chiefly of vegetables. Pork, despised beyond the level of other meat, becomes "dat" (that), a thing to point at, not to touch. What this list is meant to illustrate, however, is merely that these words and phrases are among those isolated by some Jamaicans as "Jamaicanisms" and that they are in fact words from the lexicon of Dread Talk.

Conclusion

While it is not possible to isolate any one reason for the easy spread of the Rastafarian lexicon, it is possible and necessary to look at some of the circumstances attendant on its popularity. The Rastafarian culture had, by the seventies, pervaded many aspects of the aesthetic life of the society as a whole and while the influence of the music was most powerful because it came on the airwaves many hours each day, the more visual aspects of the culture were supportive.

The Rastafari are in fact an extremely creative company of people. One cannot be sure whether this is because creative people are attracted to Rasta or because the contemplative Rasta philosophy encourages creativity or (from an economic and philosophical standpoint) because Rasta needs to make money to live and must find tasks that are not dependent on Babylon. But Rasta art, and art influenced by

---

23 Note, for example, some titles of pieces from the repertoire of the National Dance Theatre: *Two Drums for Babylon, Court of Jah,* and *Tribute to Cliff* (based on Jimmy Cliff's music).

Rasta, and Rasta influence on Jamaican popular as well as Jamaican creative dance[23] is nowhere in doubt. Davis and Simon (1977) comment that "although they are widely thought of as pariah outcasts who reject the material world, the Rastas have been the *prevailing cultural force* for twenty years, and are the major influence over young Jamaica these days" (63, my emphasis). The language of their description of societal reaction to Rasta is perhaps too strong for the eighties and somewhat more like the fifties but their perception of the point under review here is accurate. And Nettleford (1978) looking at Rasta as an appropriate response to the forces that have shaped our society says, "Small wonder that Rastafarianism now boasts great cultural clout among a groping generation of Jamaican and Commonwealth Caribbean youths in search of themselves and of a just society which they have been taught to expect but which is yet to be in their grasp. It is as though the Rasta-man is prophet, priest, and advocate – in short the society's cultural conscience" (188). The language, then, is only the most obvious manifestation of a very general and complex influence.

The philosophy of Rasta has been moving south in the Caribbean[24] and has spread as well to areas in the metropolitan countries where blacks proliferate. In other Caribbean

---

24 Craig (1980) quoting Black Stalin, calypsonian, says:
  Di Federation done dead
  CARICOM going to bed
  But di Rasta Cult spreadin(g) throughout di Caribbean
  You have Rasta now in Grenada
  You have Rasta now in St Lucia
  But to run CARIFTA we havin(g) pressure
  Now if the Rasta movement spreadin(g)
  And CARICOM dying slow
  Yes, is something Rasta know
  that politician don('t) know.

territories Dread Talk will come in contact with creoles that are different from Jamaica Creole in varying degrees. It will be interesting to see whether Dread Talk will affect these creoles in any way or whether we will be forced to see this as a phenomenon that grew up because of the particular linguistic situation in Jamaica; whether this talk is in fact "organic" to this country.

3

Rastafarian Language in
St Lucia and Barbados

alf a century after its revelation among the Jamaican
poor, Rastafari, with its distinctive way of life, has
spread to the cities of the Eastern Caribbean. Inevitably, the language that articulates the philosophy of
Rasta has spread with it. This chapter discusses the language
of Rastafari in two Eastern Caribbean territories, Barbados
and St Lucia,[1] commenting specifically on lexico-semantic
change evident in the language as it moves from the environment of Jamaica Creole to interact with the Creoles of
these two territories. A brief comment on Rastafari and on
the common history of the Caribbean is in order as a backdrop to the discussion.

Researchers have attempted to fit Rastafari into any number of preconceived frames including "political cult" (Simpson 1955), "escapist movement" (Lanternari 1963), and "messianic movement" (Barrett 1968). None of these, however,
gives a complete picture of what Rastafari is, though each
might be, like the blind men who went to see the elephant,

---

1 I wish to record here my thanks to all those whose cooperation made this chapter possible; particularly to Soucou in St Lucia and to Ikel and Adonijah in
Barbados whose goodwill gave me safe conduct throughout.

partly right. Benn's (1973) description of the Rastafari belief system as a "curious ideational synthesis … an amalgam of African cultural themes, old testament christianity and elements of Garvey's racial mystique", recognizes the multifaceted nature of the phenomenon.

It is Robert Hill (1983), however, who comes closest to pointing investigation in a direction that might be fruitful in terms of our present interest. He identifies a need "to approach the study of the phenomenon of Rastafari awakening as an integral aspect of the larger matrix of black religious nationalism, folk religious revivalism, and Jamaican peasant resistance to the plantation economy and state" (38). This kind of direction best leads to an understanding of the ease with which the Rastafarian way of life has penetrated the societies of Jamaica's Caribbean neighbours, whose histories differ from the history of Jamaica in only unimportant details. Chevannes (1980), reviewing Simpson's *Black Religions in the New World*, points to the "uniformity of the experiences of the Black Peoples of the New World" (92), and Black Stalin, the Trinidad calypsonian (himself a Rasta), describes the Caribbean people as "One race/from the same place/that make the same trip/in the same ship". Indeed Horace Campbell (1980) sees the growth of Rastafari in the Eastern Caribbean as an index, in part, of the failure of some of the popular and democratic organizations of the seventies "to root their movement in their own historical specificity" (42). The history of the islands dictates that the majority of the inhabitants are poor black people occupying underprivileged positions in societies with stark social and economic discrepancies. Such people are predisposed to accepting an ideology that offers a reversion of the social order and a positive self-image. In the case of Rasta it offers as well a deity, HIM Haile Selassie I of Ethiopia, with whose image the black self can identify, a form of worship that resembles in sound and movement[2] the Afro-Caribbean religions of the various territories, and a way of speaking that, while embodying and defining all these, easily integrates itself into the local Creoles.

The Language of Rasta-Jamaican

The language of Rastafari is Jamaica Creole (JC), the language of the Jamaican poor, "stepped up", in the terminology of one of the brethren, to reflect the philosophical stance of the Rasta man. I identify three categories of words that reflect three basic processes of word-formation within the Rastafarian lexicon (see chapter 1). The syntax of JC is left intact except for the substitution of the form "I" or "I and I" for the JC pronoun "mi".[3] The reason for this change, however, is not entirely to do with syntax. The sound /ai/ is important in the speech of the Rastafari. It is a sound with a positive force. So in one word-making process, the initial syllable in any number of words is replaced by the sound /ai/ ("I" as in I-laloo = callaloo) to form what Nettleford (1978) refers to as a "battery of 'I'-words" (201) and which leads Birhan (1981) to label the language "Iyaric". The sound /ai/ is related also to the meaning "eye", the centre of sight allowing the Rasta man to be "far seeing" when compared to the non-Rasta whose sight is at best limited ("eyes have they and see not, only Fari could see" (RMA 1976, 3; see chapter 2, this volume).

Just as sight is positive, blindness is negative and replaces the idea of seeing wherever a negative vibration is required. So, for

---

2 The Niabinghi drumming and dancing resembles the ceremonies associated with Pocomania (Jamaica). Note also the existence of Kele in St Lucia (Simpson 1977) and of Shakers in Barbados.

3 Recently the impersonal pronoun "one" appears with either the definite or indefinite article as in the sentence "I and I nah sight why a one should drink a can of orange juice when de one could sip a natural orange" (Rasta man 1978).

example "cigarette" /siigaret/ becomes /blainjaret/ "blindgarete".
This type of replacement forms the basis of another process in
which words "bear the weight of their phonological representation" (see chapter 1). A word like "oppress", as a term to
describe the action of keeping a man down, is unacceptable to
the man who feels the pressure. In Rasta it becomes "downpress" and "downpression" replaces "oppression". The English
lexicon which JC uses is in a sense brought to book in this particular process. Alleyne (1982), commenting on the list of
words so formed (Category II), says:

> As far as category 2 is concerned, the point of departure is
> the association which has already been established in
> Jamaican English (and other forms of English) between a
> certain sound sequence and a certain meaning. In other
> words, once this association is accepted, the sign loses a
> great deal of its arbitrariness and acquires some measure of
> motivation, i.e., an inherent relationship with the acquired
> meaning, akin to onomatopoeia and sound symbolism.
> Wherever the particular sound sequence occurs it must then
> convey the same meaning. (27)

His examples are "overstand" replacing "understand" and
"outformer" replacing "informer". Allsopp (1980) describes
this process as the "phono-semantic restructuring of certain
words whose outer form seems to need the kind of renova-
tion that would reflect DT feelings on certain issues with
which the words are related" (102). A more straightforward
process accounts for words that retain their English/JC forms
but change their meanings (Category I). These Allsopp
places in a semantic rather than a lexical category and
describes as "mainly SE forms with notable functional and
semantic shift sometimes plus morphological change". A
word like "chalice" falls into this category. (What used to be

a cup for administering the Holy Sacrament becomes a pipe for smoking the holy weed.) Allsopp's examples are

/faawod/ forward	to leave, depart
/babilan/ Babylon	any person seen as representative of the Euro-centred Establishment

Finally, there are new words, innovations, words whose forms are new but whose meanings, on investigation, reveal some semantic logic. This list includes /donza/ dunza or dunsa (also known as dunny) = money. For this item, Birhan (1981) gives the following etymology: "Dun is the Jamaica dialect for done and means finished, hence dunsa and dunny for money which is always too soon finished" (38).

Reggae Music and the Language of Rasta

The spread of the Rasta philosophy and the spread of the language owe much to Reggae music and the popularity of its lyrics on the tongues of its more charismatic exponents, Bob Marley, Peter Tosh, Jimmy Cliff, Burning Spear, and U-Roy, to name a few. For a proper interpretation of this phenomenon we need to be aware of the significance of music, of the word, and of the musician's role in the universe of Rasta. Brodber and Greene (1979) tell us that one of the characteristics of the theocratic world government which Rastas see as the next phase of social and political evolution is that "the singers as well as the players on instruments shall be there" (Psalm 87, v. 7), adding, "The Rastafari singers accordingly view their role as a social and religious responsibility … the singer is likely to be consciously discharging what he considers to be a socio-religious responsibility" (13). It is perhaps not by chance then that Bob Marley (1980), for example, speaks to people with a history of subjugation thus:

Emancipate yourself from mental slavery
none but ourselves can free our minds ...

The transference of philosophy and language by remote control to such a broad spectrum of society is new and could not have happened before technology advanced as far as it has today. It may be that the fact that the medium of transfer of language has been predominantly air waves rather than individual contact has influenced the processes at work and the selection of lexical items that undergo change. The preoccupation of this chapter is less with the bulk of items that have been borrowed unchanged into creoles of the English lexicon, have been translated exactly, or have been accepted as loan words into the French Creole than with the few items that have undergone lexical or semantic change with the change of environment.

Lexical Change

Hancock (1980), developing a model to describe lexical change, isolates twelve processes grouped under two main headings, "internally generated" and "externally influenced", the latter consisting of processes that "rely on resources resulting from contact with speakers of other systems" (67). Predictably, most of the items we shall examine here are the result of processes in the "external" category. Drawing on Hancock's model, I use his subcategory "Adoption" as a major category and place against it "Innovation". My present analysis retains these categories, subdividing Adoption, by far the more well subscribed, into two processes.

The total effect of Jamaican words on the language spoken by Rastas in the Eastern Caribbean has received comment in both territories under consideration. Al Gilkes (1977), writing about the speech of Barbadian Rastas, says, "Their lingo is a mixture of certain basics borrowed from their Jamaican counterparts and some of their own concoction." In St Lucia, one teacher speaks of the "infiltration of Jamaicanisms" within the speech of the Rastas.

Categories and Comment

I Adoption
a) Lexical – Phono-semantic restructuring of words

In Barbados

> /blainza/ blindza = money
> I would like to get a copy of *Calling Rastafari* everytime it comes out and just write and tell us how much it cost and how to send the "blinza" (Letter to the editor, April 1979).

Jamaican Source

> /donza/ dunza (dunsa, dunny)
> (see explanation above)

Dunza in Jamaican Rasta Talk falls within the author's list of new words (see chapter 2, this volume), innovations generated within the milieu of Rasta. In Barbados, it is an adopted Jamaican word that has submitted to the process of replacing the existing initial sound with a negative sound. So "dun" becomes "blind". This is a departure from the Jamaican process where, so far, "blind" has been used to replace word sounds involving "seeing" (e.g., siigaret). "Blindza" indicates here that Rasta perceives money as a negative thing.

> Lotal = unclean
> Any food that is not "ital" and that accounts for most of what

the normal man eats, is to the Rasta "lotal" (unclean) and not fit for human consumption (Gilkes 1977).

Jamaican Source

/aital/ Ital = vital, pure, natural, organic, food cooked without salt; Rasta food.

This word is one of the "battery of I-Words" in Jamaican Rasta Talk. "Vital" has been processed by replacing the initial sound with the positive /ai/ sound. It seems that in Barbados the normal Jamaica Creole penchant for omitting the "h" is taken for granted. Hence a hypothetical "High" tal and a negative form "Low" tal. "Low" as negative form of "high" is a logical choice and follows the pattern of one kind of process to which Rasta Talk submits JC words. Two things make the item unusual, however: the initial /h/ implication and the use of "low" instead of "blind".

It will be interesting to see how many other words will use a form other than "blind" to describe negative vibrations. I have seen "low" in one other phrase in the Barbadian corpus, "low livety" the negative opposition of "upfull livety" ("righteous living"): " 'Blindza' (money) is another agent of 'low livety' and has no place in their society" (Gilkes 1977). This process was not observed anywhere in the St Lucia corpus. While this does not necessarily indicate non-occurrence, it certainly suggests low frequency.

b) Semantic Extension – "new interpretation for an item in addition to, or in replacement of, its original one" (Hancock 1980, 74)

In Barbados

/haits/ heights = to understand
aiman haits dat = I understand

Jamaican Source

/aits/ ites = a form of greeting; the colour red

Here is a shift in function as well as in meaning. This item
takes on the function of verb in Barbados Rasta Talk. The
word normally used as a verb to mean "understand" in
Jamaica is "penetrate". The word "ites", however, is highly
symbolic in Jamaican Rasta Talk. It is more than just a greeting. Birhan (1981) defines it at length:

> Ites: Heights. A greeting wishing the person greeted to arrive
> at the heights of spirituality. Ites also means the red, which is
> the highest colour the Rastafari flag of red, gold and green as
> flown by the Niabinghi Theocracy contains. (24)

Its use here does not cause any difficulty in comprehension
for Brethren from other islands, not only because the context clues are likely to be clear but because of the high sym-
bolism of the word.

sip = to eat, drink
I sip ital (natural food) itinually (always) (Rasta man 1978)

Jamaican Source

sip = to smoke (draw on) a chalice

The semantic content here is generalized in Barbados to mean imbibing and so includes eating food cooked Rasta style.

dally = to leave (Barbados Rasta list, St Hill 1982, 35)

Jamaican Source

dally = ride; cycle; erratic movements done while riding bike

The Jamaican meaning is highly specialized. The Rasta man riding a motorcycle weaving in and out of the city traffic (dallying) daredevil style was a commonplace on the streets of Kingston in the seventies. The Jamaican equivalent of the Barbadian meaning would be "step" or "forward".

In St Lucia

/dob/ dub = to cook
aiman dob op a yood = I-man cook food (Rasta style)
evriting you duin you dobin it / dob is afrikan
"Everything you are doing you are dubbing it. Dub is African" (Young brethren from Castries, April 1982).

Jamaican Source

/dob/ dub = good piece of Reggae instrumental; flip side of Reggae 45; musical version of song usually with little or no lyrics (also: earthy dance motions with sexual suggestions, done to this music).

The meaning associated with this word in the St Lucian context marks a movement from highly specific to general when viewed in terms of the Jamaican parent form. In the comment by the young brethren that "dub is African", African, I think, merely means "black"; (in other words "dub" is a black people's word, don't expect to find it in the average dictionary).

/airashon/ Iration = cookshop; environment; dispensation (time)

A new iration Positive in vibration
Strictly Ital the man them a deal with
A place you must get to know
In Faux a Chaux gettoe
Check it out

(Advt. in *Calling Rastafari,* 1979)

Being in a Rasta iration, Soucou then asked King George to tell him about his experience as a rasta in this society over the past

(Exclusive interview with King George,
Calling Rastafari, April 1979)

"rasta woz strong doun hier / bot not nou / not in dis airashon"
"Rasta was strong down here but not now, not at this time."

(Sister at Soufriere, April 1982)

Jamaican Source

/airieshan/ Iration = creation; time

The first meaning given, "cookshop", is by far the most well documented. All over Castries are movable establishments selling ital lunches from about eleven A.M. each day. Each one is an "iration". It is possible that this meaning might have evolved from the second meaning, "environment". This could easily have meant any sort of meeting place, and since eating food cooked in a particular way is a major communal activity of Rasta, the place of the meeting could have come to monopolize the use of item. The third meaning seems to come nearest to the usage in Jamaica Talk where things happen "in this iration", creation being less the act of creation than the specific era, or perhaps better, "karma".

I am suggesting that the items in this category illustrate a process made possible by the limited person to person contact involved in the spread of this language. The words mentioned in this list are all words that appear over and over in songs and the slots they have been asked to fill are high-frequency slots. The words are symbols of Rasta activity – cooking ital food, understanding Rasta reasoning (discussion of dogma), for example – rather than examples of borrowed words with their accompanying meanings. An interesting related study might be the lyrics of the songs most popular in the territories. Two further words in the category represent a figurative level of meaning assignment, one from the St Lucia French Creole corpus, the other from Barbados.

In St Lucia

"sa *te*" = that is roots (literally "that is earth")

"Wassin", which translates literally as "roots", does exist in the St Lucian corpus with "Wassin I" a common legend on walls in the patois speaking areas. "Sa te" as an alternative, then, seems to be a conscious transfer of meaning.

Jamaican Source

"Roots" is a common item in any list of Rasta wordology. It is used as a greeting in the same way as "Ites", mentioned earlier. Birhan (1981) defines it in part as "a greeting of solidarity for Afrikan roots culture as upheld by the Rastafari. Used synonymously with Afrikan culture and with Rastafari culture" (41).

In Barbados

/dopi/ Duppy = meat; dead flesh
I nah sip duppy (anything that has to be killed before consumption)
I won't eat meat.

Jamaican Source

/dedaz/ deadahs = meat; dead flesh

This form is used in Barbados as well. "Duppy", however, is a Creole word for "ghost" or "spirit". In Barbados Rasta Talk, then, the spirit of the dead animal represents the flesh, as an alternative to the word representing simply "flesh".

II Innovation
A word that does not appear in Jamaican Rasta Talk is recorded in the corpus. (No item was recorded in this category in Barbados.)

In St Lucia

bashi = calabash; gourd

drot = meal of vegetables cooked in coconut milk (Ital stew)

aiman dob op a drot
I am cooking a drot

ombre = to be aggressive; an aggressor

all de time dem runnin down an shooting man for *ombray*
dem know de real *ombrayers* is dem big time capitalist ... I say

a minister of govament *ombraying* an other by holding de job as Sports Reporter for SLTV.

All the time they are pursuing and shooting men for being aggressive they know the real aggressors are the big-time capitalists … I say a minister of government is taking another man's bread by holding the job as sports reporter for SLTV.
(Calling Rastafari, 1979)

lak = saps, weak fellow

misye se a lak
da man de is a saps
That man is a weak fellow.

Of the words offered in this category "bashi" is the most easily traced. This seems to be a form of a diminutive of affection of the word for the calabash, a useful and easily accessible article. This particular utensil can be seen at all "irations" as large mixing and serving bowls made from sections of long oval-shaped calabashes, and as small individual eating dishes from sections of small round ones.

"Drot" (written also as jut; jot; jutt; drought) is a culinary refinement on the more general, "yuud/food". It is a dish of vegetables which must include green vegetables, cooked in coconut milk after the pattern of the Jamaican "Ital stew". I have not been able to get any explanation of its origin. It might indeed be what St Lucia Rasta Talk has made of "jorts" which appears in a Trinidad list (1981) "Wordology of Rastafari", glossed as "food".

"Lak" translates the Jamaican "saps", which describes a weak individual. One informant explains that it is a shortened form of "kakalak, the female sexual organ" so that the sentence in the example implies that the man is behaving like a woman.

"Ombre", as the example shows, is multifunctional. The informant cited above defines its verb function in this way: "to express your manhood in an aggressive way", and explains that there was a man called "Ombray" (hombre?), an aggressive type of fellow who functioned on the periphery of a group of Rastas whenever he was out of trouble/jail. His name has been applied to predatory and aggressive behaviour of the type associated with him.

Conclusion

The language of Rastafari has been dynamic enough to move outside Jamaica and to become creative/innovative in other environments. Allsopp (1980) sees this fact as indicating that it cannot be characterized as "passing local slang". It must be emphasized, he says, that "this "communolect" or "oligolect", with its many shibboleths and accompanying behaviour-patterns, has in the last ten years or so spread steadily and easily in Black communities throughout the Caribbean, whether radical (Guyana) or conservative (Barbados) almost as if these communities were linguistically pre-disposed to accommodate these unusual propensities" (103). It might thus be defended as well from the claim by some that it falls within the category "Antilanguage" as defined by Halliday (1978, 164). In fact, in Halliday's description it seems that one characteristic of the antilanguage is the narrowness of its constituency. In any case, while Rasta may be seen as a "mode of resistance" and so an anti-society spawning an anti-language, it may also be seen as "pro" a very large segment of these predominantly black communities. The following construction of "Dread" (Rasta) by one young Caribbean writer might be instructive:

The word "Dreads" as I understand it means purely, the

power that lies within any man that enables him to do or to achieve anything he wants ... To be a "Dread" therefore is to be conscious of that power, and to be developing one's power-potential for achievement ... Dread becomes therefore a philosophy of life fulfilment. (Lee 1975; also in Garrison 1979)

The language that seeks to embody all this can hardly be labelled "anti-" in its totality, even if certain aspects of its application might suggest this.

4

Dread Talk – The Speech of Rastafari in Modern Jamaican Poetry

rathwaite (1979), writing about Caribbean poetry of the 1960s, says that it released the "revelation of the word". The poet he singles out as exemplifying that revelation is Bongo Jerry, the best known of the Rastafarian poets of the sixties. And that is just, for when mention is made of the "word" in the language of Jamaica it is to the Rastafari that one immediately looks, since that group reorganized the vocabulary of Jamaica Talk to force the word to reflect a particular philosophy, a particular point of view. The requirement was for a certain consistency of meaning, and a certain relationship between sound and meaning within what has been described variously as "I-tally" (Ras Boanerges), "I-ance" (Nettleford), "Dread Talk" (Peart and Pollard), and "Iyaric" (Birhan). In the oft quoted poem "Mabrak" (see p. ix, this volume) Jerry identified the need for the use of the code of Rasta to carry the message of Rastafari, decrying the prevailing situation in which "man must use men language to carry this message". "Man" here signifies the Rasta man, the poor black man, scorned by the establishment, while "men" is not the English plural of "man" but the non-Rasta individual who represents the establishment and is identifiable in this context by his language – English.

This chapter looks at the language of Rastafari in the poetry of Jamaica, particularly at its use by poets whose regular vehicle is Standard Jamaican English (SJE) or some variety of Jamaica Creole (JC). Bongo Jerry, Dennis Scott, and Lorna Goodison are the focus of much of the discussion.

In "Mabrak", published first in *Savacou* 3/4, a volume that was to become highly controversial in Caribbean literary circles, Jerry articulated a language policy which is personal but that may be thought of as representing the feeling of a cohort of conscious young people of Jamaica during the sixties. The situation in which English, the official language of the country, is given primacy is seen as one that needs to be righted. The poet sees himself as having a mandate to change it:

> ... now I and I come to recreate:
> sight sounds and meaning to measure the feeling
> of blackhearts – alone – ...
> The coming of light to the black world. (15)

The colonial impact is identified as having its wellspring in language. Black people may try to get rid of their colonial orientation by wearing dashikis and no longer straightening their hair but

MOSTOFTHESTRAIGHTENINGISINTHETONGUE.

Bongo Jerry accuses English of deluding black people with double talk, of turning things around. The example he gives is instructive: "SAR" instead of "RAS". "Sar" is the Jamaican pronunciation of "Sir" while "Ras" is an Ethiopian royal title adopted by many Rastas; hence Ras Boanerges for example. The irony of Jerry's position becomes clear if one examines the way the speech code of Rastafari transforms words within the common pool it shares with SJE and JC, the dominant languages of the society, giving them new meanings and new significance. It is the code of Rastafari, the newcomer on the linguistic scene, that turns old meanings around.

The official language of Jamaica SJE. It is the language of formal activities in the society and of education. Jamaica Creole, the speech of the man in the street and the language of informal interaction in the society, is a creole of English lexicon; the code of Rastafari is an adjustment of the lexicon of either of these languages to satisfy certain requirements of speakers sympathetic to the philosophy of Rasta. All language within the Jamaican speech community may be described as "English related". The significance of this fact is that writers are able to include usage and meaning from within the conventions of Rasta, while writing either in English or in Jamaica Creole.

The intention behind this manipulation of words is usually to establish a kind of identification with the man at the bottom of the social ladder, the suffering Jamaican. The traditional Rasta man comes from this sector of the society. He is a "sufferer", though not all sufferers are Rastafari. Scott's poem "No Sufferer" from his collection *Uncle Time* (1973) is a good example of the use of words from the vocabulary of Dread Talk (DT) within a poem written in SJE to rationalize the inclusion of one who might be thought of as an "establishment" sympathizer within the ranks of the sufferers. Admitting that his social and economic position does not permit him to accept the label "sufferer" justly, the speaker in the poem makes a case for himself as a sufferer in a metaphorical (psychological) sense: "I have my version". The term "version" has as its primary meaning in DT the flip side of a record, usually played with instrumentals only, largely drum-like sounds. There is a pun on that word so that both the SJE and the DT meaning apply. The body of the speaker is a city in which a tortured self roams. He asks that this, his version of suffering, be recognized:

> : in the dread time of my living
> while whatever may be human chains
> me away from the surfeit of light, Mabrak
> and the safe land of my longing,
> acknowledge I. (53)

I divide the lexicon (wordology) of the code of Rasta into three categories (see chapter 1), in terms of its relation to English, as follows:

Category I   In which known items bear new meanings.
              e.g., chalice = pipe for smoking ganja

Category II   In which words bear the weight of their
              phonological implications.
              e.g., downpress = oppress

Category III /ai/ "I" words
              i. Pronominal function,
              e.g., I, I-man = I; me
              ii. Initial syllable replacement,
              e.g., I-lalu = callaloo

"Dread" is one of the more significant words in the Rasta vocabulary. It belongs to Category I in the sense that its primary meanings are not the same as those accorded it in English. As an adjective, it conveys the ultimate of either suffering or joy: good or bad. The connotations in Scott's lines quoted above are negative. The "dread" time is one in which the human being goes through extensive and intensive tribulation. Morris (1973), commenting on the use of the term in this poem, describes it as suggesting "cool anger, a sort of menacing stillness" (xx). More significant perhaps than its meaning, however, is the fact that it is used in preference to other likely adjectives ("troubled" or "difficult", for example). It signals the acceptance of the Rasta man as one unit of the manscape with which the poem is concerned. It is this man with whom the poet wishes to identify.

The use of the pronoun "I" at the end of the verse where English would expect "me" is similarly significant. For it is the Rastas who have dispensed with "me", even in the object position. "I" is used as both subject and object in Dread Talk. "I" may also be the second person pronoun translating to English as "you" singular or plural. This subcategory marks one of the few instances of the code of Rasta altering more than the lexicon of Jamaica Talk. This is interference at the level of grammar. Morris (1973) allows the following multiple significances for the last line of the quotation above: " 'I acknowledge', 'acknowledge me', 'acknowledge my Rastafarian brothers' " (xx). The preferred translation might be "acknowledge me as one of you". The term "Mabrak", Morris says, is a Rastafarian concept meaning "black lightning". Note that this term is the title word of Bongo Jerry's poem referred to.

In the poem "Solutions" from the same collection (*Uncle Time*), "I" is made to serve both SJE and DT briefly in a line where it hangs suspended like a bridge between the two:

> ... I stretch, I am
> reaching
> out, *I*
> wrench its wings into stillness. (52)

The grammar of English is not disturbed, but in the speaking of the lines the "I" in the third line, by its position at the end, by its separation from its verb, suggests an emphasis that is able to take it beyond English to Dread Talk where it would become a term of address.

Compare Scott's use of the same pronoun in two examples where there is no ambivalence, one from SJE within that same collection:

Now
heart-sailed
from home *I* name them. (6)

The other from JC from the later collection, *Dreadwalk*:

I wearing de ring dem tonight —
one gainst hate and de red pepper
tongue of malice, a snake-eye
bone-ring to touch
if *I* buck up de tempter. (44)

In these, the English first person pronoun and the Creole alternative to the more frequently used equivalent, "mi", retain their position near to their respective verbs.

The use of the Rasta "I" is perfected in the title poem of Scott's second collection, *Dreadwalk*. The strategy continues to be to end the line with that sound and to separate it from its accompanying verb. In four of the seven stanzas this usage appears. Examine the opening stanza:

blackman came walking I
heard him sing his
voice was like sand
when the wind dries it

The "I" at the end of the first line, shared between DT and SJE, allows "blackman" to be a Rasta man (in case there was any doubt): "blackman came walking I" and allows as well for the presence of his interlocutor who is not: " I heard him sing". This feature is what Rohlehr (1985) describes as the "fluid interplay of personae" (39). The poem traces a deeply philosophical discourse between two speakers, each representing a different population of the society, a different philosophical position. The future of the nation is the issue. Whoever wins will teach the children. Violence is close after the request from blackman, "give I the children". Somehow a knife is drawn but peace prevails as the interlocutor gently chides blackman for his inefficiency in handling the weapon. On the linguistic level "I" again does double duty as term of address (after "wrong") and as first person pronoun (before "said"):

> but you holding it wrong I
> said love the fist opened
> the knife fell away ...

Note that the interlocutor uses the Rasta term for peace and goodwill – "love" – to dissipate his new friend's anger. The balance maintained between the characters, the deftness displayed in handling the codes, and above it all the philosophical significance of title discourse[1] make this one of Scott's finest pieces.

The kind of manipulation of words illustrated above allows the poet to write in language that is accessible to the English-speaking outsider and to the Jamaican insider. Obviously, however, the insider here has access to far deeper levels of meaning than the untrained outsider.

It is worth noting that the category of word associated with the sound /ai/ "I" (Category III) is the most popular

---

1 For extensive commentary on this aspect of the poem see Rohlehr 1985 and Smith 1984.

category. In fact, any individual who wants to seem to be using the code of Dread easily adapts that sound to the several functions it embraces: personal pronoun (first, second, and third person), possessive pronoun and adjective, term of address and, finally, though not illustrated here, initial sound of any number of nouns. Note also that the sound is the same as that which represents the organ of sight and that "seeing" is the most highly valued sense in Rastafari theology. Alleyne (1988), commenting on the Rastafarian division of the world into positive and negative forces, says with regard to seeing: "The most positive force is perception physically realized through the eye by means of the sense of sight and leading to the metaphysical realization of the self, the ego, the 'I'" (148). And the Rasta man himself, comparing his ability to perceive with that of the non-Rasta man ("Babylon" in the code of Rasta), says "Eyes have they and see not, only Fari could see" (see chapter 2). Note the pun on "fari" which becomes both part of Rastafari and "Far eye" suggesting "far-seeing eye".

In "More Poem", from the same collection, the idiom, if not the concepts, becomes more complex as Scott exploits different categories of word together:

> … Only I-tongue have the right
> to reason, to that sense of dread.
> Man must keep silence now, except
> man without bread.
>
> No. See the flesh? It is a cave, it is
> stone. Seals every I away from light.
> Alone. Man must chant as Man can
> gainst night. (35)

The pronominal "I" of the earlier examples returns, but this time it translates into English "my". The significance of its use here is that the tongue becomes the Rasta man's tongue. Only he has the right to hold discourse about important matters, which is the force of the word "reason". It does not indicate discussion towards a logical conclusion as it might in English. Note also the pun on "I" in line two of the final stanza. From the context it is clear that "eye" is one of the intended meanings. A Rasta man might write "I" but draw an eye next to it or above it.[2] "Chant" is also used in a special way. Its meaning does not necessarily include the intoning of words after the fashion of psalms in a church service. It is allowed to mean simply "speak". The use of "man" and "dread" have already been commented upon in other contexts. The message of the lines is one of almost aggressive assertion of the right of the Rasta man (the man without bread) to speak his piece.

Like Scott, Goodison uses the code of Dread to include the Rasta man in the environment she describes and to add his particular focus or interpretation to any discourse. So words appear to mean one thing (English meaning) but in fact have at least one other meaning (Dread Talk meaning). Goodison does not restrict herself to any one category of DT word but exploits all the categories. This includes new words which might be strange in form as well as meaning to the non-Jamaican reader and which emerge as a Category IV (new items) in the ongoing analysis of DT (see chapter 2).

Goodison's descriptions have been compared to painting (Mordecai 1981), and certainly the Jamaican environment in all its diversity is graphically represented. But murals rather than simple pictures are what Goodison offers. Backdrop and foreground activity vie for the reader's attention on any one canvas. Language is one of the means of indicating the

---

2 See for example in Senya (1988, 98–9).

identity of the representatives of the different social groups interacting in the display. It is in the delicate overlap of the codes of the Jamaican speech community that Goodison excels. The poem "Ocho Rios II" from the collection *Tamarind Season*, analysed in detail elsewhere (Pollard 1991), is a good example of this. The context is a tourist city – Ocho Rios. Comments representing at least three social groups from the society are included. The poet begins the observation with the voice of the Rasta man soliloquizing:

'Today I again I forward to the sea'

The significance of the ever-present sound /ai/ "I" has already been commented upon. The first person pronoun used initially might be SJE or DT but the ambiguity is resolved by the repetition of the "I" suggesting the DT alternative "I an I". The item "forward", which in SJE is an adverb of place or a verb meaning "to send", is in DT a very positive verb meaning to "walk", "advance", "step", or simply "go". And so a line, intelligible to the speaker of English, is unmistakably a DT utterance. The Rasta man is indicating that he is visiting once more a site frequented by tourists. Later in the poem, apologizing for the poor weather, the Rasta man tells the tourist:

'… man need rain for food to grow'

and while man may include mankind in its meaning, the primary reference in this context is to Rasta man.

In another picture, an urban one from her second collection, *I Am Becoming My Mother*, Goodison describes an open market, "Bend-Down Plaza" (one literally bends down to purchase). At the end of the description the Rasta man, who in Jamaica reserves the right to have the last and uninvited word on any subject, speaks to a prospective purchaser. His voice is recognizable by the word he selects for reference to the power he worships – Jah (abbreviated form of "Jehovah"):

> Bend down nice lady
> bend down
> but try not to bend too deep
> for Jah inna this plaza
> distributing diseases
> and it look like God a sleep. (11)

Note here the juxtaposition of the Rastafarian deity Jah and the Christian God, who at the time of the comment is "sleeping". Jah threatens to give diseases to people who bend low enough to be available for carnal sin. And the God of mercy is not available to intervene.

Earlier in this poem the voice of the Rasta man is recognizable in the kind of effortless punning that has become part of his stock-in-trade. The guard, asleep with the alert guard dog beside him, is described as "a sleeping *form*" and the voice, critical of the guard's irresponsible behaviour, suggests:

> 'Dem shoulda give the dog the *uniform*.'

This poem is written for the most part in a version of JC and illustrates very well the fact that DT interacts with SJE or with JC or with both, doing what Bongo Jerry (1970) accuses English of doing: "word rearranging / ringing rings of roses, pocket full of poses" (14).

Sometimes, in order to include the Rasta man in the human environment of a poem, some lines are made to give the same meaning twice, once in SJE and once in DT. But the repetition is not obtrusive because the words are different. Category I words are useful for this exercise. For example, in the poem "Ceremony for the Banishment of the King of Swords" in her third collection, *Heartease*, Goodison uses a word from this category. Note the lines:

> ... go through this again so you can
> *penetrate* it ... (53)

In terms of SJE there is unnecessary repetition here because to "penetrate" is to "go through". But in DT to "penetrate" is "to understand, to get the full meaning of". So speakers of both codes are represented and the sentence really means "go through that again so you can understand it".

A strategy close to this one but different in its detail is used in "A Rosary of Your Names" from this same collection. God is worshipped here in a litany of fine words:

> Your names are infinity
> light and possibility
> and right
> and blessed
> and *upfull* (58)

"Upfull" is a DT term (Category IV) whose meaning includes both "right" and "blessed". The repetition is not obvious to the reader who is unaware of the code of Dread. To the initiated, however, the intention of the addition of that word to the list is the inclusion of Rastafari in this act of worship.

Equally hidden from the uninitiated is a reference to the Rasta man in one of the title poems of that collection, "Heartease I". Note the closing lines:

> Believe, believe
> and believe this

the eye know how far
Heartease is.

Here "the eye", the organ of sight, is also the Rasta individual, "the I". He is here doubly represented as the "eye"
that can truly perceive and the Rasta man who is in fact
the possessor of such an eye. This is the reverse of the
usage recorded in Scott, above, where the representation
on the page is "I".

In Goodison's first collection there is a poem that is reminiscent of Scott's "Dreadwalk". There are some differences
however. Scott, in his poem, depends chiefly on the manipulation of one item, the significant "I", to give the dimension of Rastafarian involvement. The linguistic environment
of his poem is predominantly SJE. Goodison makes use of
the "word" in a JC environment. This is in fact the more natural environment of DT, a code that arose out of a need of
the lower-class Jamaican whose language is JC to find an
identifiable voice. (Of course Scott is treating dialogue
between a Rasta man and a speaker of English.)

"The Road of Dread" (Goodison 1980, 22) might seem to
be written in JC, but if you try to read it aloud, the pauses dic-
tated by the phrasing encourage the tone and pace typical of
the Rasta man's speech. In addition, the content and the biblical references, also considered typical, mark this poem as a
soliloquy by a Rasta man walking along the road. In Jamaica
such a man is a very familiar sight and sound. The Rastafarian is known to go miles on foot conversing with himself and
occasionally shouting with much verve "Jah Rastafari!" Of
the road, the Rasta man in the poem says:

That dey road no pave
like any other black-face road
it no have no definite colour …

Pan dis same road ya sista
sometime yu drink yu salt sweat fi water
far yu sure sey at least dat no pisen,
an bread? yu picture it an chew it accordingly
an some time yu surprise fi know how dat full
man belly (22)

(That road is not paved like any other black-faced road. It has
no definite colour ... On this same road sister, sometimes you
drink your salt sweat for water for you are sure that at least
that is not poison and bread? you picture it and chew it
accordingly and sometimes you are surprised to know how
that fills your stomach.)

At the end of the road there is hope in a final stanza which
bears quotation in its entirety not only because it is valuable
as a place where the central philosophy of Rastafari is neatly
articulated but because, from the linguistic point of view, it
illustrates (in line five) Goodison's ability to move from a JC
association to an SJE association. From the point of view of
the traveller, the joy of the road of the dread, the recompense
for all the tribulation, is the meeting with a kindred spirit:

... and better still when yu meet another traveller
who have flour and yu have water and man and man
make bread together.
And dem time dey the road run straight and sure
like a young horse that cant tire
and yu catch a glimpse of the end
through the water in yu eye
I wont tell yu what I spy
but is fi dat alone I tread this road (23)

(and better still when you meet another traveller who has

flour and you have water and two people make bread together. At that time the road runs straight and sure like a young
horse that can't be made tired and you catch a glimpse of the
end through the tears in your eyes. I won't tell you what I spy
but it is for that alone that I tread this road.)

Note the almost English of the line "like a young horse that can't
tire". English might require a passive verb here but JC requires
the predicate adjective "tired". "Tire" is a fine compromise.

Conclusion

The cultural movement that is Rastafari is perhaps the boldest
statement of rejection of the values associated with European
supremacy to have been made anywhere in the New World.
Nettleford (1978) describes it as one of Plantation America's
"most authentic expressions of organic revolt in appropriate if
anguished response to some of the deepest social forces that
have shaped and still determine the discrepancies of our
Caribbean society" (188). It would be more than surprising if
the effect of the movement had not been felt in the literature
of the region. The language is the organ of the movement.

It is not the intention of this chapter to suggest that the
influence of Rastafari has been on language only, nor that
the influence has been on the work of Jamaican creative
artists only. Rohlehr's (1983) discussion is ample evidence of
the influence of Rastafari on the thought and language of
at least one non-Jamaican, Kendell Hyppolyte, a brilliant
young poet from St Lucia.[3]

The accomplishments of Scott and of Goodison must be
seen as a refinement on earlier attempts to write the Rasta

---

3 For detailed comment on influence of Dread Talk on the languages of St Lucia
see Pollard (1990).

man into the poetry of the region. Perhaps the language of Rasta had not developed enough in the sixties for non-Rastafarians to be able to manipulate it in the way these two do. Perhaps the level of understanding they have attained was not reached by the earlier writers. The fact is that if the Rasta presence may be described as "intrusive" in Scott and Goodison, it is "extrusive" in the writing of some of the earlier poets. The work of Brathwaite and McNeil provide some examples of early experimentation with the language and philosophy of Rasta. Brathwaite (1967) in "Wings of a Dove" (41) uses the "I" forms and the Dread terminology to discuss the condition of "Brother Man the Rasta man":

And I
Rastafar-I
in Babylon's boom
town, crazed by the moon
and the peace of this chalice, I
prophet and singer, scourge
of the gutter, guardian
Trench town, the Dungle and Young's
Town, rise and walk through the now silent
streets of affliction ...

Scott's "Dreadwalk" may, in fact, owe something to Brathwaite's description. Note the place of "I" at the end of the line, a feature discussed at length above. Yet there is something more convincing about Scott's lines that is not merely the result of a different craft. The single term "Dreadwalk", for example, by the time Scott published, could conjure up everything that Brathwaite's lines above describe. Equally, Goodison's description of the road of the Dread, with its weight of literal and metaphorical meanings, is capable of conjuring up a more complete picture than the "streets of affliction" from the passage above.

McNeil (1972), in his "Saint Ras" (39), says of the Rasta that he

> ... had
> not learned to fall in with the straight
> queued capitalistic for work.
> He was uneasy in traffic.

All this is contained in Scott's line

> blackman came walking I

or Goodison's

> dat de road no pave

The dramatic movement over the decade or so, which accounts for the space separating these artists as far as this influence is concerned, runs parallel to the movement within art, music, and dance as the culture of Rastafari has moved like yeast through Jamaican society, infusing all these expressions with its power.

5

The Lexicon of Dread Talk in Standard Jamaican English

The protean nature of the lexicon has been attested to in descriptions of contact between languages in varying social and political situations. Early examples abound in histories of language on the European continent. Creole languages, born of European expansion and European exploitation, illustrate the ease with which European words have fitted themselves into West African grammatical systems. The ways, however, in which languages have affected each other have rarely been examples of what speakers want to happen but rather of what has happened in spite of speakers. The often-quoted words of Dr Johnson – "to chain syllables and to lash the wind are equally the undertakings of pride" – speak to the futility of most attempts to direct the movement of words. This chapter documents in a limited way an ongoing process in which the lexicon of Standard Jamaican English, the official language of Jamaica, has been affected by the lexicon of Dread Talk, the language of the Rastafari.

Dread Talk (DT) is one of a small number of exceptional languages that have managed to direct the movement of words. It was created by the Rasta man, a member of a group with a specific history that began in the Jamaica of the 1930s.

This man saw himself as being at the bottom of the Jamaican social and economic ladder and as having a particular religion and philosophy. DT was a conscious attempt to speak in a way that could accurately describe his socioeconomic position as the man looking up from under, his religious position as a man who worshipped Haile Selassie of Ethiopia, and his cultural position as a man who adhered to certain very strict rites, including a taboo on meat. The adjustment was made to Jamaica Creole, the language of the Jamaican man-in-the-street, the major change being in the lexicon, with minor changes in the grammar.[1] In time DT became the language of lyrics accompanying much of Jamaican popular music, since the major creators of that music were from the Rastafarian community. It eventually became the language of "conscious" or of "hip" Jamaican youth.[2]

Standard Jamaican English (SJE) is the official language of Jamaica and the first language of the man at the top of the social ladder. A great social and economic gulf separates the DT speaker from the speaker of SJE. The DT speaker can be expected to try to use SJE only in a very formal situation or in one in which he is being sarcastic. The SJE speaker would use DT only in jest. It is one of the ironies of the linguistic situation in Jamaica that over the years SJE has, almost imperceptibly, absorbed several items from the "wordology" of DT, in processes of lexical expansion common in situations of language contact.

The impulse for the creation of DT, according to Brother Watu – one of the respected elders of the Rasta community in Jamaica – was not only to increase the accuracy of the words (to "step up" the language) but to ensure the secrecy of conversations which might have to be conducted in the

---

1 For a fuller description of the adjustment see chapter 1, this volume.

2 See chapter 2, this volume, for full discussion of the social history of Rastafari.

presence of outsiders. Quotations from him in "reasonings" separated by several years attest to his conviction that this was the original intention:

> so we the Rastas suppose to speak, that here, there and any-where we find ourselves, we suppose to speak and no one know what we speak beside ourself. That's how we get to start. (Chevannes 1977)

> I and I as Black People must able to stan up an talk and the Chineeman nuh hear wha we say and the Englishman nuh hear wha we say not even the Jamaican can't hear wha we say. (McPherson 1984)

But neither Brother Watu nor the congregation of the Brethren could chain the language to so small a purpose. The music of Rasta was to take it into the living rooms of the affluent young, into the schools, and, eventually, as this chapter proves, into the language of the educated minority.

Jive, the language of black musicians in the USA, had a similar intention and suffered a similar fate two decades earlier: it was absorbed into the mainstream language of white America even while prejudice against black people raged. Douglas Daniels (1985), writing about Lester Young as a word maker of the forties, quotes Connie Kay on the origins of Jive: "all the cats got a language that they talk to keep people out of their business ... There might be things you want to say and don't have no time to say it in private, so you say it so they don't – so it will go over their heads" (321). Later in that article Daniels gives some examples of words and phrases that originated with Les Young for use with his friends. One example will suffice here: "I feel a draft", which translates to Standard American English "I feel racism in our midst". The words are the same as in the Standard form but the meanings are essentially different. This process is similar to that used in the formation of DT words in Category I "in which known items bear new meanings" (see chapter 1). This is the category of word most susceptible to absorption from DT into SJE.

Signs of DT's invasion of social arenas not considered its natural place have been obvious from the seventies when young people consistently sought to "spice-up" their talk with the occasional Rasta item. In 1982 I recorded a list identified by a group of young Jamaican broadcasters as "new Jamaican words" (see chapter 2). Almost half of those words were from the vocabulary of Rasta. I noted then that the idea that Dread Talk and Jamaica Talk were becoming indistinguishable was a threatening notion to those who are suspicious of what Rasta means in the Jamaican context. In actual usage among the young, however, the one is slowly being "colonized" by the other. The examples I am about to quote are evidence that the colonization has continued and that those who are affected are no longer merely the young.

It is interesting to note that Daniels (1985), in commenting on the resemblance between Afro-American idiom and Pachuco, the idiom used by Hispanic youth of the forties, writes of the "encounter of an oral tradition with radio, jukeboxes, and phonograph records" (325). The role of popular music in the extension of Jive, Pachuco and Dread Talk beyond the narrow confines of their group into the speech of the larger community speaks to the importance of young people as agents of language change.

I have selected two items of DT to be discussed with regard to their use in SJE: "trod" and "penetrate". "Trod", the past tense form of the English verb "to tread", becomes the single form of the verb in DT and the base form in SJE. The unwary researcher might be led to see this item as an addition to the list set up by Cassidy (1971, 58) of verbs whose English past tense form becomes the unmarked form in Jamaica Creole. The verbs "lost", "broke" and "left" belong to that list. While such an analysis might identify a contributory reason and provide some reinforcement for the feature, I do not think it the main determinant since "trod" (frequently pronounced *trad*) begins to appear in both oral and written Jamaican only after the Rasta man has made innumerable journeys on foot (*traditions*) from one point of Kingston to another and has described himself and been described as "trodding down creation". Bob Marley, the king of Reggae, himself immortalized the usage in his "*Buffalo Soldier* / trodding through the land". In terms of the favouring of the form "trod" over "tread", one might want to look at other choices made within DT and hypothesize about which "word-sounds" have more power than others, bearing in mind the importance attributed to sound of words as well as of music within the culture of Rasta. Linguists might want to find out why, for example, "step" is favoured over "go", as in "I man a step" meaning "I am leaving". I believe, though I cannot as yet substantiate it, that these choices have to do more with word sound and word power than with any other influence.

Trod

Below are examples of statements including different parts of the verb "trod" with a brief description of the discourse environment of each usage.[3]

•A modern day Marco Polo *trods* Jamaican soil.

---

3 Birhan 1982 lists "trod" as noun only, an alternative to "traddition", and defines it as "the daily walk of Rastafari which is in tune with the cosmos and the creation and therefore never hurried or tense, righteous time and movament" (not paginated). Notice that in "movement" "men" is replaced by "man" because "men" is a negative sound to Rasta ears. It is not the plural of "man" but a word for the non-Rasta male as well as the homosexual.

(Headline in the *Daily Gleaner*, 24 Oct. 1985)

The *Gleaner* is the major daily newspaper of Jamaica. It is regarded by some as a bastion of formal language usage.

•Husbands have been dying and women have been *trodding* on doing their business.

(Female lawyer in luncheon conversation, 16 Sept. 1985) Although the luncheon was informal, all the participants were professional women. The language of the discourse was Standard Jamaican English.

•Since 1494 nobody ever *trodded* here.

(Male senior partner in accounting firm at informal brunch, 19 Jan. 1986)

The gathering was informal but the language of the discourse was English. It is said that men's language becomes informal more easily than women's. In this instance both men and women spoke Standard English throughout the morning. It could be that the presence of visitors from the United Kingdom and consideration for their level of comprehension affected the discourse.

•We had two hours' walk left which we *trodded* slowly.

(From short story entered in literary competition, 1988) The narrative voice in this story is English. The particular contest allows for JC only in quotations.

•We know how long he has been *trodding* here in Jamaica.

(Female director of a government agency at a book launching, 1991)

As was expected, the entire speech given by this lady was in English.

•Let us put firmly behind us the not so clean lyrics, bury the gun talk and the badman mentality, *trodding* carefully with the foreign cover versions, for obvious reasons and let's rock the globe with our music.

("Whither Dance Hall Music", by Claude Wilson, *Daily Gleaner*, 21 Feb. 1992)

Penetrate

The Concise Oxford Dictionary gives as the literal meaning for this verb "find access into or through, pass through" and as the figurative meaning "see into, find out, discern (person's mind, meaning, design, the truth)". The usage in SJE idiom tends to be the literal meaning. The DT meaning, however, is closer to the figurative meaning given in the dictionary. It signifies "to understand, think about, get the full meaning of". In the examples given below the intention is to use SJE even where the expression is not accurate. The verb in question, however, is used in the DT way. An example of traditional English usage of the item might serve to underline the DT usage in the succeeding examples. Below are three extracts, all taken from the *Daily Gleaner*. The first illustrates the traditional meaning, the others the DT meaning which is the focus of this discussion.

•Their [the Yardies] discipline is formidable making them difficult to *penetrate*.

(*Daily Gleaner*, 31 Oct. 1987)

•I explained to the doctor what the problem was but I never knew she was *penetrating* me so deep.

… did not know she was understanding me so completely.

(General Trees, DJ, quoted in *Daily Gleaner*, 11 Jan. 1988)

•The car just broke right in two. The first thing was to try and help so me stop *penetrate* the car and was about to try

and help the man …
… I stopped paying attention to the car …
   (Eyewitness report of car crash, *Daily Gleaner*, 3 Mar. 1989)

•I was late because I wasn't *penetrating* the time.
… thinking about the time.
   (Messenger to lecturer at the University of the West Indies)

The relative social positions of messenger and lecturer here indicate to this particular messenger that he should speak English. That is his intention.

Commentary

Craig (1982), quoting LePage (1960) on the differences between Jamaican English and English English, mentions eight categories of word including "words adapted to a new sense in Jamaica" (198). Christie (1982), identifying "obvious trends in relatively formal Jamaican English" (31), treats syntax and vocabulary and sees the influence of Creole and other factors. She identifies Integrative (traceable to Creole) and Innovative (not traceable to Creole) trends. Later Shields (1989), commenting on Standard English in Jamaica, discusses "changes occurring in the emergent educated variety away from what has been accepted traditionally in Jamaica as St. E" (51).

The examples of DT usage observed in SJE linguistic environments and presented in this chapter are part of the same phenomenon treated earlier by these researchers in the sense that they all describe the changing tapestry that is SJE. Hancock (1980), looking at lexical expansion in creoles, includes the process of Semantic Extension and describes it as involving "a new interpretation for an item in addition to, or in replacement of, its original one" (74). He makes a slight distinction between that and Semantic Shift, which he sees as different only in the fact that in it "the original meaning has not survived" (78). Bokamba (1982) also sees the two as being very closely related, Semantic Extension involving "adding a meaning(s) to a Standard English word" and Semantic Shift involving "the redefinition of the characteristic patterns of a word within the semantic field" (87). The process affecting the item "penetrate" falls within the former definition as an additional meaning, and that affecting "trod" within the latter in the sense that the form "tread" has largely disappeared and "trod" is no longer exclusively past tense.

Neither of these processes is unusual in the study of languages in contact. The context of Hancock's remarks is creoles, that of Bokamba is African English.[4] What makes them noteworthy in the Jamaican situation is the sociological distance between the populations that use the different codes and how unlikely one might have thought it that the influence would go in the direction described here.

The creative writers, certainly in Jamaica, have noted and made use of the changes occurring in the language. The fact that all the languages in the environment are English-related allows writers to exploit the different meanings words have for different parts of the population and the difference in words used to describe the same phenomena by different people. This peculiar situation permits an enviable flexibility within the confines of a basic anglo vocabulary. Dennis Scott and Lorna Goodison, poets who have earned both local and international reputations, have exploited the language of Rasta to a greater extent than most; Scott more the grammar than the lexicon, Goodison more the lexicon than the grammar.

---

4 See also Zuengler on Kenyan English and Bamgbose on Standard Nigerian English in Kachru 1982.

The Rasta man is frequently included in the manscape Goodison describes, through her use of his words (and not only those in the category we have so far treated). One example from her work will serve to illustrate the point. In the poem "Ceremony for the Banishment of the King of Swords", from a collection called *Heartease* (1988), the item "penetrate" immediately catches the reader's attention in a line that runs:

go through this again so you can *penetrate* it … (53)

In Standard English such a statement might be repetitive since "penetrate" means "go through". The meaning intended, however, is "go through this again so you can understand it". The DT meaning of the word is what she intends.[5] I believe that Goodison uses the word here self-consciously, as she uses other words elsewhere in her attempt to include the Rasta man in the environment she creates. This exploitation of the lexicon in the written word might well serve to reinforce the legitimization of alternate meanings within Standard Jamaican English.[6] The quotations given earlier, which are not the output of the creative imagination, represent the unselfconscious use of the words and are for this reason perhaps more significant as examples of the process that is at work within Standard Jamaican English.

---

5 For a fuller account of this use see chapter 4, this volume.
6 For an analysis of the use of DT words in the poetry of Lorna Goodison and Dennis Scott see chapter 4, this volume.

6

Globalization and the Language of Rastafari

I n the last seventy years or so, Rastafari, a new world twentieth-century socioreligious movement that spoke-first to the Jamaican poor, has spread not only to the rest of the Caribbean but outside of the region to North and South America, Europe, Africa, Asia and the Pacific. Frank Jan van Dijk (1998), in his article "Chanting Down Babylon Outernational", gives a comprehensive and enlightening review of Rastafari communities outside Jamaica. van Dijk identifies migration and travel as one route by which the philosophy of Rastafari spread but also points to radio and television waves as a means by which "the message of Jah people, cached in the powerful rhymes and pulsating rhythms of reggae, travels almost without restriction and sweeps 'Rastology' into even the remotest corners of the earth" (179). I have commented (1982a) on the relationship between the spread of the Rasta philosophy and language and the spread of Reggae music, particularly through its lyrics "on the tongues of its more charismatic proponents". Neil Savishinsky (1994), commenting on "processes relating to the diffusion and globalization of culture", points to the effect of "low cost/highly sophisticated technologies, wide-spread transnational corporate expansion, global mediaization" on the spread of the philosophy of the "Jamaican Rastafari Movement" (259). Rastafari, with its call for equal rights and justice, has easily attracted oppressed people everywhere, but it is Reggae music that has taken the message far beyond the destinations that would have been possible had the messenger been only the traveller or the migrant.[1] By the time the lyrics of Reggae music reached the airwaves of the world, the language of Rastafari had become an integral part of its culture. A code had emerged, custom made to suit the demands of the philosophy, expressing, *inter alia*, the relationship between the oppressed and the oppressor, between brethren and Babylon. Simpson, one of the earliest researchers into Jamaican religion, and indeed into Rastafari, comments that in the fifties when he was researching he did not "encounter the distinctive form of 'Rasta Talk' based on the use of the self-reflective 'I' or 'I-an-I' that is now a widely noted aspect of Rasta culture". He mentions, however, the existence of the term "Babylon" which "was used to refer to the colonial structure" (Simpson 1998, 219). Simpson's comment supports the notion that Dread Talk, a language that evolved in a self-conscious way for a specific purpose, was not born at the same time as the philosophy, the way of life, that came to be known as Rastafari. Brother W (page 7 this volume) says the code started with the desire of the Brethren to "step up" with the language and to speak in a way that would not be easily decoded by Babylon. The later objective got lost or was overtaken as the language became interesting to people outside Rasta,

---

1 See also Chevannes (1995, 269) where reference is made to Peter Lee's (1991) tribute to Bob Marley in which the love of Marley's music is seen as "the common bond linking a blues guitarist in Mississippi, a black South African soldier serving in Namibia, a young accordion player in a South African township, and a group of Australians, New Zealanders, and Scotsmen in London".

but processes had been established and the code developed and expanded with the movement and has spread with it to places where neither English nor the English-related (Jamaica) Creole (JC), which spawned Dread Talk, is spoken.

Language contact and its effects on the languages involved is an interesting and well-researched aspect of linguistics. The research focuses on how languages are altered in interactive situations in different societies, noting, for example, the categories of word that succumb most easily to change. Chapter 3 of this volume describes the talk of Rastafari adherents in Barbados, where English as well as a version of anglophone Creole are the languages of the society, and in St Lucia, where English shares the linguistic space with both francophone and anglophone Creoles. It tries to answer the question of how the language of Rastafari is transformed as it interfaces with languages outside of Jamaica.

This chapter looks at the language of Rastafari as it serves the needs of populations of different linguistic heritages. It does not (unlike the earlier chapter) comment on how the language is used in the interface between itself and languages not related to English. Instead, it examines the body of words that is available to speakers of such languages who wish to understand, perhaps eventually to use, the words Rastafarians use. To this end it comments on two dictionaries that have been offered to the global village via the Internet, using the categories established in the earlier chapters to comment on previous lists. One may regard the dictionary lists as consisting of words the Web page creators see as the minimum number of words the interested reader needs in order to have access to lyrics of songs and to other pronouncements from within the Rasta community. Far more comprehensive than either of these lists is *Rastafari and Reggae – A Dictionary and Sourcebook* by Rebekah Mulvaney. Her book includes a 95-page dictionary of words "selected for their direct relationship to Rastafari and reggae and/or for their historical value in offering a broader context from which to better understand these related subject matters" (x). This dictionary also includes, *inter alia*, names of people associated with Reggae music. However, I have chosen to focus on Web pages because they more truly represent the global village since they are immediately accessible all over the world in a way a book cannot be.

Rasta Patois Dictionary?

Dread Talk is an adjustment of the lexicon and, to a lesser extent, the grammar of Patwa (Patois/Jamaica Creole) and reflects the philosophical and religious stance of the Rastafari community, whose members see themselves as oppressed by society (Babylon, the system/shistim). So this version of Jamaica Creole (JC) might justifiably be labelled Rasta Patois and a dictionary of this language would be expected to have words used by the population that speaks patois as Rastas speak it. The two dictionaries discussed in this chapter are the *Rasta Patois Dictionary*, referred to as Dictionary 1 (D1) and the *Rasta Patois Russian Dictionary*, referred to as Dictionary 2 (D2). Both compilers have used the same thirteen sources consisting of books, handouts, notes from records, and personal information. D2 uses three additional sources. That the sources are numbered identically, with D2 adding three at the end, suggests that D2 is largely derived from D1.

Both lists go beyond the expected dictionary function by providing detail on the grammatical functions of some forms. So, for example, there is an entry "a go" in both, described in D1 (2) as "aux w/v 'going to do' as in 'me a go tell him'" and in D2 (1) as "going to do" with the same exemplifying sentence. Both regard the construction as indicating future action. Neither mentions the fact that "a + verb" expresses the continuous aspect in JC so that "me a go home" translates to English "I am/was going home".

The dictionaries include idiomatic utterances with glosses[2] as in "coo' pon", glossed as "look upon" (D1, 6; D2, 3), "everything cook and curry" (D1, 10; D2, 5), glossed in D1 as "all is well taken care of", and "mash it up" (D1, 16; D2, 10), glossed in D1 as "a huge success". This last example illustrates a slight inaccuracy. An imperative sentence is represented, in translation, by a noun phrase. In fact a more accurate translation would be "Do very well!" The sentence "We mash it up" would translate as "Our act was a huge success".

The vocabulary lists offered in the dictionaries include words that were part of JC long before Rastafari emerged in the 1930s. Some of these words came into the language unchanged from African parent languages. "Bafan", for example, is a form with both adjectival and nominal functions and comes hardly altered from Twi, one of the languages of Ghana. In both lists it is erroneously presented as two words – "bafan" and "bafang" – the one identified as noun, the other as adjective. The meanings, however, are accurate. That given for the noun (D1, 3) is the same as in the *Dictionary of Jamaican English* (DJE) (1980), "a child who did not learn to walk in the first 2–7 years", and that for the adjective "clumsy, awkward" is similar to the DJE additional meaning "A useless, clumsy person" (20). This chapter is concerned less with such words than with those that are identifiably part of the lexicon of Rastafari, those words that have been adjusted in one way or another to signal the Rasta point of view or have been created where this has been considered necessary.

van Dijk (1998) observes that "the dissemination of Rastafarian ideas and belief to Europe, the Caribbean and the

---

2 Glosses in D2 are mostly in Russian. Comments here are restricted to those that are also given in English.

Pacific gave rise to an extremely heterogeneous countercul-
ture". What he sees as constant, however, are the "social,
political and cultural ideas associated with the movement"
(194). Hepner (1998), commenting on the same notion of
heterogeneity within a more limited geographical area, notes
that the one theme that remains unchanged whether the
Brethren speak in Jamaica or North America is the "militant
rejection of Babylon" (210). It is the language of Rasta, Dread
Talk, that is used to articulate the common sentiments. Hutton and Murrell (1998), restating a point made by Nettleford
three decades earlier, comment that the Rastas "in their self-
affirmation ... have gone beyond the use of African names
and linguistic adaptation to actual language creation. That is,
they have created a language with its own vocabulary, much
of which was never encountered before in Jamaica" (50).

Word-Making Processes

All living languages are dynamic. Accordingly the language
used by Rastafari is constantly evolving within identifiable
categories defined in the earlier chapters of this collection.
There are four categories resulting from four processes of
word formation. A theory informs each process. The process
itself, however, once understood, can be applied without a
knowledge of the theory. Let us examine first the process gen-
erating the I-words (Category III), the category most commonly recognized as Rasta words. Behind the strength and
importance of these words is the power of the sound /ai/ "I".
This is the same sound heard in /aiman/ I-man, /aianai/ I-an-
I, /diai/ the-I, all of which represent first and second person
pronouns, both singular and plural, and in /ai/ "eye", the
organ of sight. A pun on "eye" recognizes "fari" (far-eye) in
the third and fourth syllables of Rastafari as the "far-seeing
eye" (discussed in chapter 2) so important in Rasta philosophy.

Words receive a certain elevation by being brought into this category, which has proved easy to manipulate. Schoolboys in the seventies, for example, anxious to identify with Rasta before they could understand (overstand) its philosophy, could make use of this category the way their grandparents used Pig-Latin/Gypsy in elementary schools of yesteryear.[3] This ease of manipulation perhaps accounts for the fact that the lists include a relatively small number of these words. Any such list can be extended by simply replacing the initial syllable of a given noun with "I" (so for example "apple" would become "I-ple"). There are some words that begin with the sound associated with the letter "y" rather than "I", such as "yude"/food (page 48 this volume). D2 (16) would include "yod"/trod, "yound" /sound, "yunder"/thunder in such a list.[4]

Sound is paramount in Dread Talk, and "wordsound" is a seminal concept. Consistency in sound and meaning is also highly valued. Category II consists of English words that have been adjusted to relate sound to meaning. For instance, the word "up", which indicates a direction that is usually positive, must be used consistently to indicate something positive. Thus the word "oppress" cannot be used to express its conventional meaning in English as pronunciation of the first syllable indicates upward movement, which contradicts the indication of downward movement in the second syllable. So the often-quoted "DOWNpress" replaces OPpress (UPress). Similarly overstand replaces UNDERstand.

There are certain English words that are considered negative by Rastas and wherever they occur the meaning is

---

3 For a discussion on Gypsy see Aceto (1995).

4 I have some difficulty recognizing these, especially "yod", since "trod" is a particularly well-used item in the Rasta vocabulary. For a full treatment of this item see pages 89–92.

negative. "Blind" is one such word. It is in opposition to "see," which is particularly positive because of its relationship to the organ of sight. So "cigarette", which is a negative item, becomes "blindjarete" (page 8 this volume). Equally negative words are "hate" and "dead" These have to be replaced with positive words. So DEADline becomes LIFEline and DEADicate becomes LIVIcate. To manipulate this word formation process correctly, however, the speaker needs to be aware of certain pronunciations common in Jamaica, particularly the addition of the "h" before vowels in a random list of words or syllables and its omission in an equally random list. The Barbadian Rastas, hearing Jamaicans pronounce "ital" with an initial "h" ("hightal") to describe clean, Rasta-approved food, invented the opposite "lotal" to describe unclean food (see page 59), thus introducing a Barbadian Rasta item which would not be generated in Jamaica where people who say "hightal" automatically write "ital". D1 and D2 both include "apprecilove" which is what "appreciate" becomes when the negative "hate" in "apprecihate" is replaced with the positive "love". D2 includes "argumant" which replaces "argument" since the form "men", which in Dread Talk means "homosexual", must always be avoided in a movement that views homosexuality negatively within a Jamaica that is distinctly homophobic.

Category I words, where known English items are given new meanings, are also presented in the lists. Some of the most important words in the Dread Talk vocabulary fall within this category. "Babylon" has already been mentioned as the term for the establishment, recognized by Simpson as having existed from the earliest days of the movement. "Dread" soon came to mean a person with (dread) locks, a Rasta man, as opposed to a "baaled"/bald-headed and clean-shaven and so non-Rasta man. Additional meanings for "dread" have come to include possible meanings of the word in English. The following are offered in D1 (9) where the word is both noun and adjective:

1 a person with dreadlocks
2 a serious idea or thing
3 dangerous situation or person
4 the "dreadful power of the holy"
5 experientially "awesome, fearful confrontation of a people with a primordial but historically denied racial selfhood"

Another word in Category I is "red", which becomes not only a colour but a modifier meaning "very high on herb" (D1, 20). "Herb" is marijuana, sacred to the Rastas as the herb of the sacrament. This plant itself is referred to by a multiplicity of names, one of the more popular being "Collie weed". This term is rendered "Kali/Cooly" in D2 (9). (The second spelling here should be avoided since it might lead to the unlikely pronunciation "coolie".) There is also "Lambsbread" (D1, 16) which refers to a particularly high quality of marijuana (this is given as Lamb's Bread in D2, 10), "sinsemilla; sensie" glossed (D1, 22) as "popular, potent, seedless, unpollinated, female strain of marijuana" (see also D2, 14). Another Category I word is "chalice", the pipe for smoking marijuana. This might be considered a natural transfer from the chalice, the cup of the Eucharist in the Christian church. Other names for it are "cutchie" (D1, 8; D2, 4) and "chillum, chalewa" (D2, 3; D1, 5), all of which fall within Category IV: New Items.

New Items refer to words created by Rasta. "Spliff", the term used for the herb when it is rolled (prepared like a cigarette), falls within this category (D2, 15; D1, 23). Some others are "deaders" for meat and its by-products (D1, 8; D2, 4), discussed in some detail in an earlier chapter (page 50); "Elizabitch" (D2, 5), which expresses a particular attitude to

Queen Elizabeth, the reigning monarch of Great Britain (a person much hated by Jamaican Rastas, second only to the Pope of Rome); "livity" and "upful", which are treated as synonyms in D2, although in fact the former is a noun, the latter an adjective glossed as "positive; encouraging" in D1 (25); and "Niaman; Rasta man" (D1, 17).

Process and Theory

I mentioned earlier the existence of a theory or rationale behind word making processes. An example of what happens when the process is used without an understanding of the rationale is the unlikely entry "Niamen" in D2 (11). For reasons explained above, the term "men" is stigmatized and it would be sacrilege to attach it to a word that is an alternative for Rasta man. American pronunciation of the word "Niaman" might have caused the confusion here. Another unlikely creation is "lovepreciate" which appears in D2, 10. Perhaps a "new Rasta" tried to make a word without an understanding of the rationale – the notion of eliminating negative sounds. "Apprecilove" is legitimate, "lovepreciate" is not. This is easily shown by pronouncing it as LOVEpreciHate and noting the inherent contradiction.

Word-Making Processes Revisited or Discourse on Origins

With the spread of the lyrics of Reggae songs and so of the language of Rastafari, interest in the theories behind the formation of words has grown and thinkers both inside and outside the movement have applied various levels of logic to the emergence of the different categories of word. Predictably, Category III, the "I-words", the most distinctive feature of the code, has received the most attention. Here are some recent comments on that feature. Hepner (1998) quotes Brother Judah, a New York Rasta man, member of the Twelve Tribes of Israel, who explains the use of the pronominal "I-an-I" in this way: "we refer to one another [other Rastas] as 'I-an-I' – we don't make no one a second person. We don't say 'I and him' or 'us'. We just say 'I-an-I' because every person is a first person" (211).

Edmonds (1998) reasons as follows: "Since 'I' in Rastafarian thought signifies the divine principle that is in all humanity, 'I-an-I' is an expression of the oneness between two (or more) persons and between the speaker and God (whether Selassie or the god principle that rules in all creation)" (33). On the preference of the subject pronoun "I" in both subject and object positions where JC uses "me" he says: "Rastas use 'I-an-I' (as subject even when the sentence calls for an object) to indicate that all people are active, creative agents and not passive objects."

Mulvaney (1990) gives a slightly different explanation for the same phenomenon: "Rastas believe 'me' connotes subservience or objectification of the human individual whereas 'I' is thought to emphasize the subjective and individual character of a person" (39).

Defining "I and I" Mulvaney writes: "Both singular and plural pronoun in Rasta language. As singular, the speaker chooses I and I to signify the ever presence of Jah. As plural, the choice of I an I signifies the existence of a spirituality and metaphysically intimate relationship among the speaker, other individuals present or spoken of, and Jah" (39).

McFarlane (1998), in his discussion of the epistemological significance of "I-an-I", describes the form as the "self-reflexive use of the subject pronoun" and sees the "I" words as "the means by which Rastas make all informed utterances related to their principles, cultic practices, and self affirmation" (107). He reaffirms the link identified by earlier researchers,

Yawney for example (page 28 this volume), between the "I" words and the "I" in "Jah Selassie I, previously known as Ras Tafari" and both to "'the word made flesh' of early Christian theology" and to the early Rastas (punning) reconfiguration of the title as Rasta-for-I. In McFarlane's discourse the "I" that ends Rastafari is the first principle of Rasta life "which reverses the order of things to make the last first and the first last" (108).

Notably absent from any of these descriptions is the connection between the eye, the organ of sight, and the first person pronoun and the effect of that convergence of sound on the power behind the "I" words, although this was a point emphasized in earlier research. Perhaps this omission is a warning that something is changing. What is added to the discourse and what gets lost is unpredictable. It could be that as the research moves further and further away from Jamaica, the locale of the beginnings of the movement and the home of some of the oldest interviewees, emphases change. What is clear is that interest in the culture and so in the language of a movement that speaks to oppressed black people, and eventually to the oppressed of all races, is not waning. In fact, the Rastafarian language may well become increasingly entrenched in other communities, since language is one outlet of defiance that the oppressor is unlikely to succeed in frustrating.

This chapter has focused on word lists provided in the global media by Rasta Patois dictionaries and does not say anything about how the code functions in its interaction with languages with which it comes in contact. It would be interesting to note, for example, which words are accepted unchanged into these languages and which are translated. Questions such as the acceptance/rejection of the principle of word sound need to be examined in conjunction with the question of how heterogeneous the culture is outside Jamaica. Dread Talk in the French and Spanish Caribbean and in Latin America immediately offers itself for future study. In the seventies the Rastafari culture spread to Cuba, Jamaica's nearest neighbour, taken there both by travellers and by Reggae music. In a recent presentation Davis Furé (1999) spoke about Cuban youth and the influence of Reggae, hip-hop, and other imported lifestyles, which he says are quickly adapted to the new context. With regard to expression among the youth he indicated that certain adjustments have had to be made in a situation where Rastas, for example, are using Spanish to discuss an imported topic with a foreign vocabulary. He commented that the process was yielding "something new and different" and used the term *transculturación*.

Indeed *transculturación* is an excellent term to describe the feature of Rastafari with which this chapter began – the spread of its culture to all the continents and its influence in these new lands. The variations inherent in such a spread (the heterogeneity of which van Dijk and Hepner write) are part of what Davis Furé describes as "something new and different". This phrase is reminiscent of "something torn and new" that Edward Brathwaite (1969), writing three decades earlier, used to describe the rhythms of the steel pan, a metaphor for the new Caribbean man: "now waking / … making / with their / rhythms some- / thing torn / and new" (113). Perhaps a new Rasta man, or several versions of such a man, is emerging.[5] And perhaps several versions of the code will emerge to express the new realities.

---

5 Jan deCosmo, in a recent presentation, described the Rastafarian community in Bahia, Brazil, and pointed to variations on the Rastafari theology as it interacts with fundamentalist Christian beliefs. See also Neil Savishinsky (1994, 1998) on Rastafari in the Pacific and South Africa.

That dey road no pave
like any other black-face road
it no have no definite colour
and it fence two side
with live barbwire.

And no look fi no milepost
fi measure you walking
and no tek no stone as
dead or familiar

for sometime you pass a ting
you know as ... call it stone again
and is a snake ready fi squeeze yu
kill yu
or is a dead man tek him
possessions tease yu
Then the place dem yu feel
is resting place because time
before that yu welcome like rain,
go dey again?
bad dawg, bad face tun fi drive yu underground
wey yu no have no light fi walk
and yu find sey that many yu meet who sey
them understand
is only from dem mout dem talk.
One good ting though, that same treatment
mek yu walk untold distance
for to continue yu have fe walk far
away from the wicked.

Pan dis same road ya sista
sometime yu drink yu salt sweat fi water
for yu sure sey at least dat no pisen,
and bread? yu picture it and chew it accordingly
and some time yu surprise fi know how dat full
man belly.
Some day no have no definite colour

no beginning and no ending, it just name day
or night as how you feel fi call it.

Den why I tread it brother?
well mek I tell yu bout the day dem
when the father send some little bird
that swallow flute fi trill me
And when him instruct the sun fi smile pan me first.

and the sky calm like sea when it sleep
and a breeze like a laugh follow me.
or the man find a stream that pure like baby mind
and the water ease down yu throat
and quiet yu inside.

and better still when yu meet another traveller
who have flour and yu have water and man and man
make bread together.
And dem time dey the road run straight and sure
like a young horse that cant tire
and yu catch a glimpse of the end
through the water in yu eye
I wont tell yu what I spy
but is fi dat alone I tread this road.

LORNA GOODISON, 1980

Bibliography

Aceto, Michael. 1995. "Variation in a Secret Creole Language of Panama". *Language in Society* 24.

Albuquerque, Klaus de. 1977. "Millenarian Movements and the Politics of Liberation: The Rastafarians of Jamaica". Doctoral dissertation, Virginia Polytechnic Institute and State University.

Alleyne, Mervyn C. 1982. "The Epistemological Foundations of Caribbean Speech Behaviour". Inaugural lecture (typescript), Faculty of Arts, UWI, Mona, Jamaica.

– 1988. *Roots of Jamaican Culture.* London: Pluto Press.

Allsopp, R. 1980. "How Creole Lexicons Expand". In *Theoretical Orientations in Creole Studies,* edited by A. Valdman and A. Highfield, 19–107.

Barrett, Leonard T. 1968. *A Study in Messianic Cultism in Jamaica.* Caribbean Monograph Series No. 6. Rio Piedras: Institute of Caribbean Studies, University of Puerto Rico.

– 1977. *The Rastafarians: Sounds of Cultural Dissonance.* Boston: Beacon Press.

Benn, Dennis M. 1972. "Historical and Contemporary Expressions of Black Consciousness in the Caribbean". MSc thesis, University of the West Indies.

Birhan, Iyawta Farika. 1981. *Iyaric – A Brief Journey into Rastafarian Word Sound.* (Pamphlet.)

– 1982. "Linguistic Language Latitudes – The Queen's 'English' and the Emperor's 'Iyaric'". In *Itations of Jamaica and I Rastafari.* New York: Ragner and Bernhard.

Boanerges, Ras. 1984. "Now We Shall Be a Nation". *Youth Black Faith* 1, no. 1.

Bokainba, Eyamba G. 1982. "The

Africanization of English".In *The Other Tongue: English across Cultures,* edited by B. Kachru.

Brathwaite, Edward [Kamau]. 1967. *Rights of Passage.* London: Oxford University Press.

– 1969. *Islands.* London: Oxford University Press.

– 1974. "The African Presence in Caribbean Literature". *Daedalus* 103, no. 2: 73–109.

– 1977a. *Mother Poem.* London: Oxford University Press.

– 1977b. "The Love Axe/1: Developing a Caribbean Aesthetic 1962–1964", *Bim* 16, no. 61.

– ed. 1979. *New Poets from Jamaica.* Mona, Jamaica: Savacou Publications.

Brodber, Erna, and J. Edward Greene. 1979. "Roots and Reggae – Ideological Tendencies in the Recent History of Afro Jamaica". Paper presented at the Conference on Human Development Models in Action, Fanon Research Center, Mogadishu, Somalia, June.

Campbell, Horace. 1980. "The Rastafarians in the Eastern Caribbean". *Caribbean Quarterly* 26, no. 4.

Cassidy, Frederic G. 1971. *Jamaica Talk.* London: Macmillan Education.

Cassidy, F.G., and R.B. LePage. 1980. *Dictionary of Jamaican English* (2nd ed.). Cambridge: Cambridge University Press,

Cambridge. (First edition 1967.)

Chevannes, Alston Barrington. 1971. "Jamaica Lower Class Religion: Struggles against Oppression". MSc thesis, University of the West Indies, Mona, Jamaica.

– 1976. "Social Origins of the Rastafarian Language". Manuscript.

– 1977. "Era of Dreadlocks". Paper presented at the Conference on the African Diaspora, Hampton Institute, Virginia.

– 1979. "Social Origins of the Rastafari Movement". Mimeo.

– 1980. Review of *Black Religions in the New World* by G.E. Simpson (1977). *Caribbean Quarterly* 26, no. 4.

– 1995. *Rastafari: Roots and Ideology.* Syracuse and Kingston, Jamaica: Syracuse University Press and The Press, University of the West Indies.

Christie, Pauline. 1982. "Trends in Jamaican English: Increasing Deviance or Emerging Standards?" Paper presented at the Fourth Biennial Conference of the Society for Caribbean Linguistics, Suriname, September 1982.

Count Ossie. 1972. (Interview with Elean Thomas.) "Groundations – Count Ossie and the MRR". *Swing,* Sept/Oct: 10–11.

Craig, Dennis R. 1980. "Language, Society and Education in the

West Indies". *Caribbean Journal of Education* 7, nos. 1 & 2.

– 1982. "Towards a Description of Caribbean English". In *The Other Tongue: English across Cultures,* edited by B. Kachru.

Daniels, Douglas. 1985. "Lester Young: Master of Jive". *American Music,* Fall 1985: 313–28.

Davis, Stephen, and Peter Simon, 1977. *Reggae Bloodlines.* New York: Anchor Press.

Davis Furé, Samuel. 1999. "Rastafari and Popular Culture in Contemporary Cuba: A Case Study of Caribbean Connections". Presentation at the Twenty-fourth Annual Conference, Caribbean Studies Association, Panama City.

DeCosmo, Jan. 1999. "A New Cristianity for the Modern World: Rastafari Fundamentalism in Salvador, Bahia, Brazil". Presentation at the Twenty-fourth Annual Conference, Caribbean Studies Association, Panama City.

Edmonds, Ennis B. 1998. "Dread 'I' In-a-Babylon: Ideological Resistance and Cultural Revitalization". In *Chanting Down Babylon,* edited by Murrell, Spencer and McFarlane.

Edwards, Adolph. 1967. *Marcus Garvey.* London: New Beacon Publishers.

Elkins, W.F. 1977. *Street Preachers,*

Faith Healers and Herb Doctors in Jamaica. New York: Revisionist Press.

Garrison, Len. 1979. *Black Youth, Rastafarianism and the Identity Crisis in Brit*ain. London: ACER Project.

Gilkes, Al. 1977. "For 'I and I' ". *Nation,* 13 Feb. 1977.

Goodison, Lorna. 1980. *Tamarind Season.* Kingston, Jamaica: Institute of Jamaica.

– 1988. *Heartease.* London: New Beacon.

Halliday, M.A.K. 1978. *Language as Social Semiotic: The Social Interpretation of Language and Meaning.* London: Arnold.

Hancock, Ian. 1980. "Lexical Expansion in Creoles". In *Theoretical Orientations in Creole Languages,* edited by Valdman and Highfield, 63–88.

Hartman, Ras Daniel. 1972. Interview. *Swing,* May: 35.

Hepner, Randal L. 1998. "Chanting Down Babylon in the Belly of the Beast: The Rastafarian Movement in the Metropolitan United States". In *Chanting Down Babylon,* edited by Murrell, Spencer and McFarlane.

Hill, Robert. 1983. "Leonard P. Howell and Millennarian Visions in Early Rastafari." *Jamaica Journal* 16, no. 1.

Hutton, Clinton, and Nathaniel Murrell. 1998. "Rastas' Psychology of Blackness".

In *Chanting Down Babylon,* edited by Murrell, Spencer and McFarlane.

Jerry, Bongo. 1969. Taped recording of a "reasoning" and poetry reading session at the University of the West Indies (Mona). From the collection of Edward Brathwaite.

— 1970. "Mabrak". *Savacou: Journal of the Caribbean Artists' Movements,* no. 3/4: 13–16.

Kachru, Braj, ed. 1982. *The Other Tongue: English across Cultures.* Urbana, Ill.: University of Illinois Press.

Kitzinger, Sheila. 1969. "Protest and Mysticism: The Rastafari Cult in Jamaica". *Journal for the Scientific Study of Religion* 8, no. 2: 240–62.

Lanternari, V. 1963. *The Religions of the Oppressed.* Translated from the Italian by Lisa Sergio. London: McGibbon & Kee.

Lee, Robert. 1975. "The Dread – A Caribbean Experience". *West Indian World,* 21 March.

— 1991. *Guitar Player*, May: 82.

Marley, Robert Nesta (Bob). 1980. "Redemption Song". On *Uprising* (LP record album). Kingston, Jamaica: Tuff Gong.

McFarlane, Adrian. 1998. "The Epistomological Significance of 'I-an-I' as a response to Quashie and Anancyism in Jamaican Culture". In *Chanting Down Babylon,* edited by Murrell, Spencer and McFarlane.

McNeil, Anthony. 1972. *Reel from "The Life Movie".* Kingston, Jamaica: Savacou Publications.

McPherson, Ras E. 1984. Transcription of "Reasoning" given by Ras Boanerges/Bongo Watu, Oct. 1982. Reprinted in *Youth Black Faith,* circular no. 1.

Mordecai, P. 1981. "Wooing with Words – Some Comments on the Poetry of Lorna Goodison". *Jamaica Journal* 45.

Morris, Mervyn. 1973. Introduction to *Uncle Time* by Dennis Scott (1973). Pittsburgh: University of Pittsburgh Press.

Mulvaney, Rebekah. 1990. *Rastafari and Reggae – A Dictionary and Sourcebook.* New York: Greenwood Press.

Murrell, Nathaniel, William David Spencer, and Adrian Anthony McFarlane. 1998. *Chanting Down Babylon.* Kingston, Jamaica: Ian Randle Publishers.

Nettleford, Rex M. 1970. *Mirror Mirror: Identity, Race and Protest in Jamaica.* Kingston, Jamaica: Collins and Sangster.

— 1978. *Caribbean Cultural Identity: The Case of Jamaica.* Kingston, Jamaica: Institute of Jamaica.

Owens, Joseph. 1976. *Dread – The Rastafarians of Jamaica.* Kingston, Jamaica: Sangster.

Peart, Joshua. 1977. "Dread Talk". Undergraduate paper presented in Caribbean Study, UWI,

Mona, Jamaica.

Pollard, Velma. 1978. "Code Switching in Jamaica Creole – Some Educational Implications". *Caribbean Journal of Education* 5, nos. 1 & 2.

– 1980. "Dread Talk: The Speech of the Rastafari in Jamaica". *Caribbean Quarterly* 28, no. 4: 32–41.

– 1982a. "The Social History of Dread Talk". *Caribbean Quarterly* 28, no. 4: 17–40.

– 1982b. "The Speech of the Rastafarians of Jamaica in the Eastern Caribbean – The Case of St Lucia". Paper presented at the Fourth Biennial Conference of the Society for Caribbean Linguistics, Suriname, September. Reprinted in *International Journal of the Sociology of Language* 85 (1990): 81–90.

– 1989. "Dread Talk – The Speech of Rastafari in Modern Jamaican Poetry". Paper presented at the Association of Commonwealth Literatures and Languages (ACLALS) Silver Jubilee Conference, University of Kent, Canterbury, 24–31 August. Reprinted in Anna Rutherford, ed., 1992. *From Commonwealth to Post-Colonial.* Denmark: Dangaroo Press.

– 1990. "The Speech of the Rastafarians of Jamaica in the Eastern Caribbean – The Case of St Lucia". *International Journal of the Sociology of Language* 85: 81–90.

– 1991. "Mothertongue Voices in the Writing of Olive Senior and Lorna Goodison". In *Motherlands – Black Women's Writing from Africa, the Caribbean and South Asia*, edited by S. Nasta, 238–53. London: The Women's Press.

Post, Ken. 1970. "The Bible as Ideology: Ethiopianism in Jamaica, 1930–1938". In *African Perspectives,* edited by Allen and Johnson, 185–207. Cambridge: Cambridge University Press.

Rastaman. 1978. "Rastas and the Bible". *Nation,* 21 July.

Rasta Patois Dictionary. Updated 1996, www.eng.miami.edu/~kbrown/rasta-la.htm

Rasta Patois-Russian Dictionary. www.zhumal.ru:8085/music/rasta/patois.html

Rastafari Movement Association (RMA). 1976. *Rastafari: A Modern Antique.* Kingston, Jamaica: RMA.

Rodney, Walter. 1969. *The Groundings with My Brothers.* London: Bogle-L'Ouverture Publications.

Rohlehr, F. Gordon. 1969. "Sounds and Pressure: Jamaica Blues". *Moko,* nos. 16 & 17.

– 1971. "Some Problems of Assessment: A Look at New Expressions in the Arts of the Contemporary Caribbean". *Caribbean Quarterly* 17, nos. 3 & 4 (Sept./Dec.): 72–113.

– 1985. "The Problem of the Problem of Form". *Caribbean Quarterly* 31, no. 1.

Savishinsky, Neil J. 1994. "Traditional Popular Culture and the Global Spread of the Jamaican Rastafari Movement". *New West Indian Guide* 68, nos. 3 and 4.

– 1998. "African Dimensions of the Jamaican Rastafari Movement". In *Chanting Down Babylon,* edited by Murrell, Spencer and McFarlane.

Scott, Dennis. 1973. *Uncle Time.* Pittsburgh: University of Pittsburgh Press.

– 1982. *Dreadwalk.* London: New Beacon Books.

Senya. 1988. *Senya Poems.* Frederikstad: Ay Ay.

Shields, Kathryn. 1989. "Standard English in Jamaica: A Case of Competing Models". *English World Wide* 10, no. 1: 41–53.

Simpson, G.E. 1955. "The Rastafari Movement – Political Cultism in West Kingston". *Social and Economic Studies* 4, no. 2.

– 1970. *Religious Cults of the Caribbean.* Institute of Caribbean Studies. Rio Piedras, University of Puerto Rico. Chapter 3: "The Rastafari Movement – Political Cultism in West Kingston, Jamaica"; chapter 4: "The Ras Tafari Movement in Jamaica in Its Millennial Aspect".

– 1977. *Black Religions in the New World.* New York: Columbia University Press.

Smith, Ian. 1984. "Poetics of Self – Dennis Scott's Dangerous Style." *Caribbean Quarterly* 30, no. 1.

Smith, M.G., R. Augier, and R. Nettleford. 1960. *The Rastafari Movement in Jamaica.* Kingston, Jamaica: Institute of Social and Economic Research, University of the West Indies.

Soucou. 1979. "Exclusive Interview with King George". *Calling Rastafari*, April: 3

St Hill, Margaret V. 1982. "The Speech Patterns of the Rastafarians of Barbados". Undergraduate paper presented as Caribbean Study, UWI, Cave Hill, Barbados.

Stalin, Black. 1979. "Caribbean Unity". On *To the Caribbean Man* (LP record album). Port of Spain, Trinidad: Wizard Productions.

Valdman, A., and A. Highfield, eds. 1980. *Theoretical Orientations in Creole Studies.* New York: Academic Press.

van Dijk, Frank Jan. 1998. "Chanting Down Babylon Outernational: The Rise of Rastafari in Europe, the Caribbean, and the Pacfic". In *Chanting Down Babylon,* edited by Murrell, Spencer and McFarlane.

White, Garth 1967. "Rudie, Oh

Rudie!" *Caribbean Quarterly* 13
(3), 39–44.

Yawney, Carole. 1972. "Herb and
the Chalice: The Symbolic Life
of the Children of Slaves".
Paper presented at the annual
meeting of the Caribbean
Sociology and Anthropology
Association, Montreal.

– 1970. "Remnants of All Nations:
Rastararian Attitudes to Race
and Nationality". In *Ethnicity
in the Americas*, edited by F.
Henry. Mouton: The
Netherlands.

Zuengler, Jane. 1982. "Kenyan
English". In *The Other Tongue:
English across Cultures*, edited by
B. Kachru.